K.G. Confidential

A Festschrift for Katherine Gallagher

KG Confidential first published 2015. All rights reserved.

Published by Circle Time Press, London
info@circletimepress.co.uk

The right of each of the poets to be identified as the author of their work has been asserted by them in accordance with the Copyright, Designs and Patents Act 1988.

Printed in Great Britain by Imprint Digital, Devon.

Design and Typesetting Laura Alvarado.

Funded by the Menzies Centre for Australian Studies, Kings College, London and by the contributors.

ISBN 978-0-9564082-3-5

Cover design by Tim Butt.

For Katherine Gallagher: poet, translator, teacher, poetry activist and friend.

Contents

Introduction	1
Keeper of the Illusion, *Shanta Acharya*	3
Kangaroo, *Robert Desnos / Timothy Adès*	4
Katherine's Publisher, *Arc Publications*	5
Beauty Sleep, *Allen Ashley*	6
Wattle Time, *Anna Avebury*	7
Pausing, *Yvonne Baker (Govan)*	8
Apology from a Reluctant Tortoise, *Anne Ballard*	9
Emotional Trajectories, *Michael Bartholomew Biggs*	10
Queen Katherine, *Liz Berry*	11
Katherine, Our Friend, *Barbara Bevan*	12
Katherine at Railway Fields, *David Bevan*	12
Time Zones, *Rosemary Blake*	13
Wheal Coates, *Ed Briggs*	14
The Quiet Day, *Sara Boyes*	15
Parakeets Settle in the Suburbs, *Maggie Butt*	17
Katherine, Palmers Green and Poetry, *Joanna Cameron*	18
Katherine as Teacher, *Rev Franco Cavarra*	19
Reading the 40 rules of love… , *Kay Cotton*	20
Five Quatrians for Katherine, *Martyn Crucefix*	21
Abide With Me, *C.L. Dallat*	22
The Gardener, *Valerie Darville*	23
The Wenlock Poetry Festival, *Ross Donlon*	24
Trailblazer, *Penny Dopson*	25
The Sweeper's Tale, *Sarah Doyle*	26
At Readings, *Jane Duran*	27
From Little Acorns, *Margaret Eddershaw*	28
Katherine at Barnet, *Pam Edwards*	29
North Ferriby Foreshore, Remembering, *Roger Elkin*	30
Garden Walk , Garden Portrait, *Diane Fahey*	31
Roses, *Anthony Fisher*	32
Katherine as Tutor, *Rosemary Fisher*	33
Parallel Process, *Viv Fogel*	34
Eucalyptus Marginata, *Sandy Fitts*	35
Electric Psalms, *Kate Foley*	37
Touchstone, *Lindsay Fursland*	38
Drafting, *Ruth Hanchett*	39
First Flight Lift off, *Gwen Hartland*	40
Out to Lunch, *Joy Howard*	41
55 Douglas Road, *Sonia Jarema*	42
Spelling Katherine, *Mimi Khalvati*	43

And, *Angela Kirby*	44
To the Blue Gum, *Kaye Lee*	45
The Policeman's Secret Notebook, *John Mackay*	46
Unarranged, *Tracey Martin*	47
In Praise of Lazy Rivers, *Nancy Mattson*	48
At the Lifeboat Station..., *Mary Michaels*	49
Sprouts, *Joan Michelson*	50
Kennings for Katherine, *Cheryl Moskowitz*	51
Here & There, *Paul Munden*	52
Katherine's Interview, *Elena Nistor*	53
Sonnet for Katherine, *Les Murray*	55
Zigzag Thinking, *Anmarie Nicholson*	56
A Calculation of Dark, *Ruth O'Callaghan*	57
This Instant, *Jan Owen*	58
tab 12, *Laurie Evan Owen*	59
Katherine and Acumen, *Patricia Oxley*	60
Field Cricket and Poetry, *William Oxley*	61
The Other Side of the Bridge, *Dorrie Pearton*	62
Barrier, *Mario Petrucci*	63
Young Katherine Meets..., *Peter Phillips*	64
Travelling Companions, *Harriet Proudfoot*	65
Cycle Race, *Tom Roberts*	66
Wake, *Fiona Sampson*	67
For Katherine, *Marina Sanchez*	68
Katherine's Red Beret, *Daphne Schiller*	69
Katherine, *Myra Schneider*	70
Les Salines, Normandie, *Penelope Shuttle*	71
In Celebration, *Maggie Scott*	73
In Flight, *Gordon Simms*	74
The State Collection, *Jocelyn Simms*	75
Nestlings, *Belinda Singleton*	76
The Reindeers' Revolt, *Hylda Sims*	77
My Katherine, *Anne Stewart*	79
Dear Muse, *Christine Vial*	80
For Katherine, *Rita Walsh*	80
Katherine Gallagher's Poetry, *Dilys Wood*	81
Intarsia, *Wendy Wright*	83
In Company of Camels, *Anne Woodford*	85
Speedwriting, *BA Zanditon*	86
Katherine, *Patricia Zontelli*	87
Lost Property, *Veronica Zundel*	88
Contributors	89

Introduction

Festschrift, from the German: fest – celebration, schrift – writing.
A celebration in writing and, in this case, of writing.

This celebration is in honour of **Katherine Gallagher**, or KG as she often calls herself. Katherine is a much-loved Australian poet living in London, whose poetry, translation, teaching and tireless work on the poetry scene has inspired this anthology. She left Australia to escape an unhappy love affair, and ended up winning the hearts of all the contributors to this book – and many more besides.

She is a truly international presence, frequently reading in the UK, France and Australia. Her poems have been published in French, German, Hebrew, Italian, Romanian and Serbian and she translated Jean-Jacques Celly's poems from French to English in *The Sleepwalker with Eyes of Clay* (1994).

Her first collection, *The Eye's Circle*, was published in Australia in 1974, followed by a pamphlet, *Tributaries of the Love-song*, 1978, and *Passengers to the City*, 1985. In the UK she has published *Fish-rings on Water*, 1989, *Finding the Prince*, 1993, a haiku collection *Shifts*, 1997 and *After Kandinsky*, 2005. Her most recent, and highly acclaimed, full collections are *Tigers on the Silk Road*, (2000) *Circus-Apprentice*, (2006) and a 'new and selected' collection *Carnival Edge*, (2009) – all published by Arc.

Katherine's famous sense of humour and wide-awake attention to the detail of the world have also found an outlet in her wonderful poems for children, which are included in almost 40 anthologies. Her understanding of children was enhanced by a B Ed, five years teaching in two Melbourne high schools, and teaching English in Paris during the 1970s. Settling in North London in 1979, she taught in various London schools and has maintained her strong connection with children and young people through radio broadcasts and numerous workshops across the capital. She has also judged the children's section of the Barnet poetry competition for more than 21 years.

Her wide-ranging work on the poetry scene has included tutoring for the Open College of the Arts, running regular workshops at Jackson's Lane and Torriano and many other venues, being an active member of the National Association of Writers in Education and Second Light, and working at Poetry London and Writers Inc/Blue Nose Poets. She founded the vibrant Palmers Green Poetry Society Stanza Group in March 2007, co-ran the Stevie Smith Festival and co-runs Poetry in Palmers Green. She has been a Writer in Residence and a Poet in Residence, and has won awards and fellowships including the Warana Prize, a Royal Literary Fund bursary and a London Society of Authors' Foundation Award.

She has judged many poetry competitions and read at numerous poetry festivals. Somehow, in addition to all this, she finds the energy to loyally attend readings of tutees and friends, and it is always a joy to see one of her distinctive hats coming through the door, because, more than anything, Katherine is loved.

Contributors to the anthology have sent emails with messages including:
"She is my hero."
"I wouldn't have done any of this without her."
"...one of the nicest and most supportive women in the poetry world."
 "She is a subtle and brilliant poet whose warmth, integrity and
passionate commitment to her craft have been truly inspirational."
"She not only inspires and encourages, while modestly making barely any mention of her own achievements, but has a rare generosity of spirit that brings great loyalty, harmony and affection."
"Katherine has been a long-standing support and influence on my poetry. I admire her work greatly and am delighted to have been given a way of expressing this."
"She has nurtured so many of us in her incomparable way."

Admiration for her determination to bring poetry to places where it may not be expected, for poetry as a way of life, is echoed in many of the poems and contributions.

The title of the book *KG Confidential* comes from the subject line
of the email which winged its way across continents to secretly request contributions. Her husband Bernard and son Julien have also helped.

The 80+ poets and friends featuring in this anthology represent a cross-section of established and new writers, from Australia, France, Romania and the UK. The contributions are arranged alphabetically by author – an egalitarian approach which I think Katherine will approve. It is noticeable how many of the poets return to the themes of birds and gardens, picking up Katherine's love of the natural world, but also her own alert, bird-like qualities and the way that she, as gardener, nurtures and grows new poets.

This anthology is dedicated to the gifted poet, the incomparable, irrepressible KG, from all of us.

Maggie Butt (editor)
London 2015

Keeper of the Illusion

She takes her countries as they come,
drying to dust the spent tongue.

Having swallowed universes,
they sit quietly inside her,
tracing sky-splitting poems, sculptures

for all weathers. The human voice her canvas –
words floating, flaring, extravagant as flowers.

Letting us see the connection between things,
a true witness, her steady lines build bridges
moulded out of the earth's surprises –

a sea that cannot be mapped,
guarding an inner music,
a flute-voice reaching towards newness.

The purpose of arriving among words,
where language has changed, where we have changed,
is to get a taste of everything.

Life distilled into light refracts a dream
spellbound by the limitless –
a cathedral about to lift the world off its knees.

This country we keep coming back to
walks us home, makes us look inside ourselves.

We know our road home is written
in the language of astonishment –
our feet facing all ways into the poem!

Shanta Acharya

Note: I have borrowed phrases from Katharine Gallagher's poems - it is my tribute to her.

Le Kangourou

Kangourou premier, roi des Kangourous,
Ayant accroché son grand sabre au clou
S'assoit dans un trône en feuilles de chou.

Sa femme arrivant, pleine de courroux,
Dans sa poche a mis ses fils et ses sous,
Ses gants, son mouchoir et ses roudoudous.

Kangourou dernier, roi des kangourous,
Avait les yeux verts et les cheveux roux.
Sa femme peignait son royal époux.

Kangourou le Roux, roi des Kangourous,
Kangourou dernier, Kangourou le Roux.

The Kangaroo

Kangaroo the First, King Kangaroo,
Hung on a hook his huge skean dhu,
Sat on a throne, in leaves of callaloo.

His wife turned up, she was in a stew,
Pocket full of joeys and a penny or two,
Her gloves, her hanky and her candy chew.

Kangaroo the Last, King Kangaroo,
Eyes green as grass, hair of rust-red hue,
She combed her husband, as queens may do.

Kangaroo of rust, King Kangaroo,
Kangaroo the Last, he's rust-red too.

Robert Desnos translated by Timothy Adès

from the book *Storysongs/Chantefables*, Agenda Editions,
Éditions Grund and Timothy Adès.

Katherine's Publisher

Katherine is the sort of poet that every publisher loves to publish – a talented writer with a wide appeal who abounds in energy and enthusiasm, is a keen yet modest promoter of her own work, and who understands (more than most) the poetry publisher's uphill task.

Our first encounter with Katherine was at Compendium Bookshop in the mid-1990s where we'd launched, among other titles, *Mother Tongue*, a selection of the poems by the Austrian poet Rose Auslander in a translation by Jean Boase-Beier and Anthony Vivis. Katherine harangued us mercilessly about not including the poems in the original German alongside the translation in our edition, and although we tried to counter her criticism, it certainly set us thinking. And indeed, not long after, we made the decision to publish all our translations (and now there are over 90 of them) as bilingual editions.

A few years later, we became acquainted with Katherine's own work when we received the manuscript of *Tigers on the Silk Road*, which we published in 2000, and since then we have published two further collections, *Circus-Apprentice* and *Carnival Edge*. Our association with Katherine over fifteen years has been a very happy one. Not only has it seen the publication of three fine collections, but many readings and workshops, all of them delivered with a great deal of thought and professionalism. Her generous nature manifests itself not only in how she has always been prepared to 'give things a go' as far as her publishers are concerned, but also in how she goes out of her way to promote other poets and bring them into the limelight. We are proud to publish you, Katherine.

Tony Ward & Angela Jarman
Arc Publications

Beauty Sleep

To wake
from a hundred years of bliss,
to this?

Disturbed,
to dreams I can't return –
a shame.

The prince,
as ugly as a wart,
to blame.

He fought
his way through bush and briar.
But why?

Reward –
a marriage is proposed.
Must I?

I'm trapped!
My fate it has been sealed:
a kiss.

To wake
from my lengthy beauty sleep –
to this?

Allen Ashley

Wattle Time

Today, for you, in a distant land,
a certain tree is greening.

Spring is coaxing golden buds
open, spilling sweetness like sunshine
over miles of bush. Golden-haired,
the wattle is waking, shaking
her tresses free from winter's grasp.

Nor drought, nor fiercest fire
can do her harm. Her seeds sleep,
dreaming, even in scorched earth,
biding their time, rising
each September, a burnished
phoenix, green and gold.

Anna Avebury

Pausing

Your stillness might be because you are content
to stand in this narrow hallway, with the dull sheen of its floor;

to look out from the archways, which shelter its in-between space,
echo the shape of the window across the street, limit your gaze.

Or it may be that your thoughts are elsewhere
and, for the moment, your maid and child are bystanders,

their chatter fading, as the quietness from the house pools
in the slow light, while you catch the sun on your apron.

Perhaps you are considering how your future is behind you,
enclosed in a state of grace in the well-swept courtyard,

where pale plants inch from the border onto the paving stones?
To want more than this you might lose all you hold dear.

Or are you thinking about the blue arc of the sky,
with its endless possibilities? If only you would step forward.

(After 'A Courtyard in Delft', Pieter de Hooch)

Yvonne Baker (Govan)

Apology from a Reluctant Tortoise

Today I waddle without ease or grace:
Seated, I prop my left leg on a chair.
I have to walk at half my normal pace.

When I backed off that train, plus heavy case,
The platform I expected wasn't there.
Today I waddle without ease or grace.

My leg descended into hyperspace
Then clashed with some sub-carriage ironware
So now I walk at half my normal pace.

My calf resembles mauve and yellow lace,
My shin is swollen like a conference pear,
Which makes me waddle without ease or grace.

From toe to knee, I have a carapace
Of white stretch bandage, which I hate to wear:
It slows me down to half my normal pace.

It was my fault, a truth I have to face:
A bit less hurry and a bit more care,
I'd not be waddling without ease or grace:
Nor forced to walk at half my normal pace.

Anne Ballard

Emotional Trajectories

you are my gravity's other edge – from Katherine Gallagher's poem *'Circus Apprentice'*

Planets curve in orbits under forces
of attraction. Lovers trace two courses –
both eccentric – round one proposition
we're in love, and may reach opposition:
if a full diameter divides them
empty darkness, stretched between them, hides them.
At his perigee – when he's most close to
focussing on her – she's not supposed to
be so distant.
              Apogee's a chance
for looking back on what should be a dance
and not a race. Don't Newton's laws ordain
that if one waits the other one must gain?
So time itself, in time, can synchronize
their passions with each sunset and sunrise.

Michael Bartholomew-Biggs

Queen Katherine

My favourite memory of Katherine is one which celebrates her inherent queenliness!

My first pamphlet had its launch in a packed little room in London Bridge. It was a warm summer night and everyone had to sit on the floor as there was only one chair. Katherine had winged it down from Palmers Green and when she arrived in the midst of the introductions my publisher Les immediately pulled out that one lone chair, a very grand office armchair, and sat her upon it. It seemed to me a perfect sight: Katherine perched regally on her throne offering her blessings to my poems and the start of my life as a poet. She had welcomed me into her North London Stanza as a new and very green writer and shown me kindness and encouragement ever since. Her support and endless enthusiasm for poetry, coupled with her wonderful wit, make her a gracious and brilliant force for good.

So we honour you, dear Katherine, queen amongst North London poets! Long may you reign!

Liz Berry

Katherine - Our Friend

Katherine has been a close friend for over 30 years. Our boys have grown up together and are still friends. She has been through some of life's difficult times with me - always with a supporting hand. Her love of poetry has enthused all our meetings and I know she has encouraged many others.

My husband and I have enjoyed Katherine and Bernard's company so many times. I include her as part of the family. Always cheerful and kind, age rests so lightly on her.
–Many great days!

Barbara Bevan

Katherine at Railway Fields

In the spring of 2002 Katherine was appointed Writer in Residence at Railway Fields, a nature reserve in Harringay, North London. More than 1500 children from local schools visited the site every summer. Katherine worked with the children, ran poetry workshops for adult visitors and, at the end of her stay, composed a characteristically lyrical poem about the reserve and its wildlife.

Katherine's energy and creative flair illuminated her residency and introduced both children and adults to a new way of responding to the natural world. As the Council's conservation officer, based at Railway Fields at the time, I was struck by Katherine's close rapport with the children and how she encouraged them to read aloud their charming compositions. It was an unforgettable summer as Katherine's poem 'Summer Odyssey' from *Circus-Apprentice*, Arc Publications, 2006 records.

David Bevan

Time Zones

At Sydney's Botanic Gardens
elm, oak and ash are bare, wintering
with swamp-mahogany and Norfolk Island pine.

What were we thinking of, back then.

You're quiet, you say.
I worry when you're quiet.

Beyond Circular Quay, gulls follow the wake
of mainland ferries, or float alongside on the drifts of air.

It's years now since we saw the headlands at the entrance
to the harbour, or walked where tea-tree and Casuarina
grow so casually along the boulevards.

Driving at night through bush: the small blue light
of high-beam pulses faintly on the dash-board.
The smell of gum-trees fills the open windows.
Our headlamps light the white leaves by the roadside.

Rosemary Blake

From *Wintering,* (Ekstasis Editions, 2007)

Wheal Coates

Dad says We won't find it, they've taken it down.

He kicks the tussocks, crushes
ling underfoot, anxious to touch
the bedazzlement of old stones, re-live

time, half a century and more ago.

Fence stakes, rusting strands of barbed wire
delimit the old mine land. Ridge summit
– we were approaching too obliquely –

and there's the calciner stack.
Used to remove sulphur and arsenic,
straight and defiant of the cliff edge,

it defines the clear blue sky, resists the Atlantic.

Rich and large was the mine, a many-acred sett,
lode beneath the sea, men and materials caged
underground through shafts, unfathomed crush,

the tin stream refined to liquid,
paid to bounders, pumped into receivership.
Dad's in the Towanroath, uncapped

in light and shadow while I aspire

to the Florentine apertures, archways, tall, slender,
whose granite is soft in the lowering September
sun, grazed with iron ore and copper.

Back with our lucky bunch of ling, we pass a marooned boy
playing by a smoke-tinted city jeep. He's marking time
kicking a ball round the car park now it's emptying,

headers full of winning teams, cups and hero shirts.

Ed Briggs

The Quiet Day

For Katherine, in celebration of the many things you do for poetry: classes, workshops, leading groups, readings and, of course, writing poems that bring people and places, especially Australia, so strongly to life.

Inside it is quiet. We are told
speaking will be on the subject of prayer;
meditation may kindle our love.

The courtyard, filled with grass,
today will do as a heart. Or is it a soul?
"The thing which does not exist."

What is clearly visible is the holly tree:
it fills one corner, is of medium height,
a dark bitter-green. It is berry-less.

What is not quiet is the holly tree;
a great noise draws me to it. Inside
it pulsates with sparrows chirping and singing.

There are small ones, plump ones,
soft ones, slender ones,
some are marked strongly, some are dun-coloured.

They dance up and down
their claws holding on, shifting along
and they flutter their wings, they chirp and sing.

Covering the bush is chicken-wire netting:
a sanctuary has been made;
there is access and exit, but a slim narrow one.

Bags of nuts hang down,
there is a tray of sand, high up, and seeds.
The sparrows fly out but they come back.

This holly tree spreads; it becomes
the courtyard, the time of day, the people.
It is as if the holly tree is aflame.

It is as if – on this quiet day –
the holly tree, pulsating with sparrows,
does as a soul.

Sara Boyes

Parakeets Settle in the Suburbs

For dear Katherine, who flew in like a parakeet, set up home like a bower bird and sings like a nightingale, leading our dawn-chorus.

An emerald flock flashes out
lasooes the rooves of London
imported spice from paradise
flavour of dubloon, lagoon;
close to the airport, escapologists
multiplying in the wing-wide air.
No notion yet if they will turn
grey squirrel, knot-weed, mink
or if their tropic lime will blend
with cricket pitch and oak
viridian and verdigris
forest groves of Arden, Sherwood,
chord a bright note of light
in all the greens of England.

Maggie Butt

From: *Lipstick*, (Greenwich Exchange, 2007)

Katherine, Palmers Green and Poetry

Katherine knocked at the door of the Palmers Green Bookshop in late 2000. It was at closing time and, typically, she did not give up but tapped very gently and smilingly at the door to ask myself and my mother about our interest in poetry events. From that moment (and through a similar connection forged with Myra Schneider) poetry blossomed again in Palmers Green. The Stevie Smith festival took on both a life of it's own and a quirkily hopeful, irrepressible quality that was pure Katherine. After events at the bookshop ceased seven years later, Poetry in Palmers Green was set up and is still thriving, thanks to a lively committee, devoted friends and the hard work and enthusiasm of Katherine and Myra.

I went to a reading of Katherine's at the Poetry Cafe and was entranced by this small, determined, funny and feminine woman, this world traveller, art lover and intellectual, a bridger of different worlds, Australia, Europe (France especially!), a teacher, a campaigner, a Londoner, recognized as a sincere and enthusiastic member of her local community.

Many have defined the qualities of her poetry, my personal view of it, and her, is this:
Katherine is an encourager, both as a friend and a teacher, she is essentially concerned with articulating (without sentimentality and with awareness of life's sadness and injustices) the celebration of this beautiful, fragile and mystical human life and the natural world that has born us (and born with us). Differing from Stevie Smith obviously in life experience, and in the emphasis placed on celebration of life, they share an interest in the life of the spirit and a healthy lightness of touch belying a powerful intellectual grit. I recommend Katherine's paper on Stevie delivered at the festival in 2002 and shockingly still not published! A worthy successor indeed, she never tires of quoting 'poetry is a strong way out'.

If I was to attempt a haiku about Katherine it would go something like this; she dashes in, a hint of perfume, words tinkling, eyes twinkling, small feet determinedly dancing forward...

Joanna Cameron

Katherine as Teacher

It was the Modern History class at Newlands High School in Melbourne's northern suburbs where I first got to know Katherine Gallagher in 1964. I was a sixteen year old new student from a Catholic college and Kath had just been appointed to the staff.

Despite our common religious identity we rarely discussed religious issues then, but the questions that our reading was raising in that class. What immediately impressed me was her passion to stimulate the imagination in arriving at some sort of explanation of what had taken place and why. Having just emerged from a fairly strict and unimaginative school environment, I found those classroom debates and discussions interesting, challenging and inspiring all at the same time.

Under Kath's encouragement, I began to reach out and try all sorts of creative activities that had remained suffocated and buried deep inside of me. It was with Kath's prompting and infectious optimism that I became involved in the Debating Society, the school newspaper, the Film Society and all those activities just waiting to be let loose. Later on as a student at the University of Melbourne, I kept in touch and we became good friends. Once established in my career as a stage director of opera and drama, Kath the poet was always an inspiration to embrace and confront the new despite the very real difficulties involved. We continued to keep in touch whenever I found myself in London and always looked forward to an evening as a guest of Kath, Bernard and Julien.

When late in life, I finally decided to study for the priesthood, Kath was one of the ones who encouraged me to follow that particular call whatever the cost and its considerable uncertainties. With Kath as a mentor and guide, I came to the realisation that being true to one's unique identity would always involve a cost but that the price was always worth paying. To use Manning Clark's often quoted category, Kath is most definitely one of those "enlargers" of life for whom we continue to be forever grateful.

Fr Franco Cavarra

Reading the 40 Rules of Love at Baker St.

I'm swept up in the crush hour
over the line
                              into the tube
nose against a neck in a moleskin jacket; no sweat.

At Oxford Circus, eyebrow touching a small blue
butterfly hair-slide on a fresh-faced blonde,
breathing the exhalations of fourteen commuters
I'm knocked out   (Mind The Gap)
by a head twitching like a cow ridding itself of flies.

                              'Don't worry'
says a voice from the other side of the world
as an oaken branch bursts buds in my face

'It's a tree, not a gun. Hold on
We're going up the escalator.'

The tree begins to spread   a sound of wings
and all the birds of Australia come to roost:
catbirds, figbirds, the warblers and the pippits,
cassowaries, frogmouths and kookaburras
are settling in   to raise the roof.

Kay Cotton

Five quatrains for Katherine

I watch you walk out
on the east-running road just as far
as a field of sunflowers
the tarmac bisects

where all day south
their open faces follow the light
so to your left
they blaze before you

while to your right
they have turned cold green shoulders—
you won't go far
not just your eyes full

you turn back now
to consider the west
filled with feathers of purple cirrus
where two contrails

cross like a clue
you've no need of now the angles are clear
and no more to do
you set it down

Martyn Crucefix

Abide With Me

After the global climacteric,
the four-minute warming, the drought
and construction of great silver towers
for the final, essential distillation,
I loaded my mountain-bike panniers
with Accrington honeydew melons
and Forthriverbed tangerines,
pedalled my way across rocky
escarpments and gulches to forty-
one North, fifty-twenty-
two West and clambered aboard.

Most days I spend in the shade;
there is much to explore
and the pantries have yielded up
marmalade, beans and dried fish.
But by evening I take Uncle Wallace's
Edison cylinder phonograph
up to the boat deck and listen
to 'Bunker Street Rag' and his
favourite Wesleyan hymn,
while somewhere beyond Nova Scotia
the unsinkable giant sends signals
I choose to ignore in the dark.

Steerage, as usual, are the last to find out.

C. L. Dallat

'Abide With Me' was one of the first pieces I brought to Robert Greacen's late-80s Notting Hill workshop (soon to become Matthew Sweeney's Dombey Street group when Robert retired to Dublin). The crucible of much 'nineties 'new-gen' poetry, I relished evenings there not just for first sight of some great poems I still treasure but for the critical advice I received and for the company of poets. Katherine Gallagher was a mainstay of that company and I came to value her poems, her advice, and her knowledge of poetry and of London's poetry scene, as activist, catalyst and, for us, enthusiastic supporter of all that I, and my wife, Anne-Marie Fyfe, have done over the years since (both poetry-wise and arts-business-wise) especially as Katherine's been a regular attendee and much-appreciated guest reader at Anne-Marie's Troubadour poetry events since the mid-'nineties. A moving and perceptive poet in her own right and a vital and energising presence in the world of poetry!

The Gardener

(Inspired by Jo Shapcott's 'The Governess')

Unminded, he watches. The mistress in her silks and laces,
walking in her rose garden. And the governess,
sewing all that hot afternoon. And the child with her.
To the mistress he is a tree or a decorative shrub,
clipped to the rough likeness of a man.
Or an ornamental statue, a fountain perhaps.
He sees her drinking tea on the terrace with her guests,
and watches through windows as they dine.
Sparkling jewellery, and candles and silver plate.
And him in the dark. And he has seen her also,
in the shadows of the lawn when the master was from home.
The governess is her alter ego, grey to her white,
useful to her idleness. Frustrated in her barrenness,
she stitches her life on to sheets, while the child sleeps.
Red on white, with the scent of herbs around her.

Valerie Darville

The Wenlock Poetry Festival

After Breughel

As though gravity had suddenly become horizontal
patrons run from the town square, pulled by the magnet of poetry.
Arms point, faces gawk, legs buck
as they try to run in different directions:
a woman abandons her corset of couplets;
a man fears for his post modern codpiece;
girls and boys laugh at the upturned town
as they gaze through words to new worlds;
Wenlock Books strains at its spine;
Anna is multi-armed deity, books wave in each hand;
money clutchers quiver with reader fever;
the moon jumps over a cow;
Christopher Robin jumps out of the closet;
Poet Laureates dance with Parrot Lorikeets;
Owls and pussycats busk with The Jumblies.
Barrels of ballads roll down to pubs already awash with sonnets.
Titania and Oberon agree on the weather for just three days
while Puck trails stars above the Much that is Wenlock.

Ross Donlon

Trailblazer

That day I stumbled on you for the first time
at the Great Bed of Words, a last minute thing,
a day trip to explore unfamiliar wordscapes,
my ticket for the afternoon session; chose you.

You with your swag bag of ideas,
opening up new territory as we raked the past,
other poets; your blue eyes lit up,
insightful towards the horizon.

And today I walk for the first time
into your Mother's Garden, as much English
as antipodean and you here in London
still digging, the gleam of your gold shining.

Penny Dopson

The Sweeper's Tale

It settles in miniscule drifts, colourful
as fairy-wings, and twice as fragile.
Sometimes, the wind takes it, peppering
pavements with specks of blue, pink, silver.

Horseshoe...

Skittering across church-steps, treading
a lucky path. Fortune. Favour. Tiny
paper facsimiles of their iron counterparts,
a U-shape made to hold promises.

Bell...

Music peals, vibrating a soundscape,
ripples of celebration spreading
irresistibly outwards. Rise, descent,
rise, descent. A ring for a ring.

Loveheart...

Two curves, rounding, combining,
coming to the same point: a single
meeting place in the soul's geometry.
Hearts given and held and cherished.

Bow...

Loose ends reach to fold back on each other,
as knots are tied in never-ending loops.
Ornament and substance. Fibre enfolds
fibre in a lifetime's embrace.

Horseshoe, bell, loveheart, bow...
I sweep the confetti that settles, like snow.

Sarah Doyle 2015

Pubished in *Petals in the Pan,* (Kind of a Hurricane Press, 2015.)

At Readings

Perhaps we know each other
best in our poetry – passing
and greeting at readings

in the Art Workers Guild
or at Torriano in the grand John Rety days
when you read 'Lonesome Tonight' –

'I watched him throw old dancing partners
shoulder-high and wished for someone
interested in books. Why me?'

and I read 'Boogie Woogie' –
a wallflower with sad bony shoulders
and pale lemon shoes.

How good it is to listen and be there!
And always a sympathy, a warmth,
stopping to chat for a few moments

among the poets and the poems.

Jane Duran

From Little Acorns

After KG's *'Year of the Tree'*

Given your affinity with trees
ability to put down tenacious roots,
becoming an oak
is an evolution you hardly notice.
You do wonder why your glossy hair
floats and whispers
with no sign of a breeze,
you are curious about the titmouse nest
in your coat-pocket,
another clue: Athena's owl
shivers feathers on your shoulder,
one day you look down
to see serrated fingers.

After forty years as genus quercus
round your bole scatters
a fine crop of acorns
sprouting a tiny forest;
your canopy offers
shelter from storms
shade in harsh sunlight,
you teach them
how to yield when gales blow
sway with the swell of birdsong
shed withered leaves
capture in their miniscule cups
the sweet sap of your wisdom.

As your protégés grow
they strive to emulate
the generosity of your branches
ambition of your green shoots,
every day they chant in chorus:
Long live our great oak!
But be assured
no-one will ever count your rings.

Margaret Eddershaw

Katherine at Barnet

A very big thank you to Katherine for advising and judging Barnet Open Poetry's Junior section for 21 years, which called for a special celebration.

Photographs by Anthony Fisher

Katherine has been a stalwart, supporting the junior sections of Barnet's Open Competition since it began in the 1990s.

The competition was supported by Adrian Benjamin at All Saints Church in Whetstone, who arranged to publish an anthology of the winning poems each year, which poets may illustrate themselves, and so we have a colourful archive.

Katherine does much to encourage the young entrants at the annual prizegiving at The Bull Theatre in Barnet, advising and commenting on their work.

Pam Edwards BEM
Hon Secretary
Barnet Borough Arts Council

North Ferriby Foreshore, Remembering

i.m. Granddad Charles and Peter Reading who never met

Not sand, but reaches of mudflat
veined by rainbowy seawater-seeps
along the Humberside strand. And,
further out, a pewter gleam where
the Trent – water within water –
fattens to estuary's broad blade, then
wider still, circle-swirls to mouth
at silent horizons, the North Sea,
Europe and beyond.

Seems worlds away from Trent's
well-head and its insignificant sibilants
trickling through Bailey's farmyard.

How memories tumble. To hills.
And home: the moorland village
cricked safe in England's vertebrae
where gritstone walling collects
the fields' purposes.

And to Granddad – simple man
crowned local bigwig – mouthing down
his home-grown workmates,
Thait senatucked.*

Laugh at that. That bastardised Latin
he hadn't even had chance to learn
let alone forget, any more than he'd
heard of Ferriby. Or estuary.
Though knew belonging,
like the sons of his name.

Roger Elkin

* North Staffordshire dialect for you are sinew-tight; exhausted.
Peter Reading's poem, 'Dog's Tomb', (Untitled, 2001) contains the lines, "QVI CAECVS ET SENECTVTE CONFECTVS, Who blindness and senility prepared".

Katherine awarded the poem as 1st Prize in the Segora Open Poetry Competition, 2012, at St Clementin, where I was pleased to meet up with her (and again in 2014, and hopefully next year!) so it has significance and fond memories for both of us.

Garden Walk

A stand of ivory irises, gold-tongued,
cinerarias in royal velvets.
We pass my father's camellia tree,
its yield of coral cups the first since his death.
Long years. You call it 'the miracle tree'.
Nearby, this mandala bloom: splayed petals
frame the abounding heart, heart-red.

I think of these hopeful, circumspect days
as your harvest won from pain endured;
this garden, your own small share
of life's quest for beauty in survival.
At dusk, whether we listen or not,
bird songs will wreathe this old house in splendour.
Later, lotus-stars on a black pond.

Garden Portrait

My mother, side-view, under the moonah tree

There's a plainness to inner nobility,
a listening calm won from grief mastered.
So, in age, your profile portrait
comes into its own: pared down, refined,
telling a life through flesh and bone.
You sit, no viewer in sight,
looking at hazed light while looking within –
as into a tarn cupped by mountain
depths: lens to hawk, cloud, starburst.
What would I need to know, to wear sunlight
as richly, sparsely, as you do now:
your face tilted to receive the wind's balm;
that look of earthed serenity; body
poised as a cormorant's, wings outstretched.

Diane Fahey

Roses

You speak of pruning, black spot, dead-heading.
Mention of floribunda, standard, climbing.
We've a dog rose hanging with honeysuckle.

Roses grow in exotic places, Turkey, Russia, Persia,
where at the perfect moment five tonnes of flowers
are crushed to yield one litre of oil.

It's easy to characterise it's composition -
eugenol, farnesol, geraniol, linalool, nerol,
nonylic aldehyde, rhodinol, sterophene.

Can I tell you how its fragrance affects me
so you can feel as I do, the spin of colour,
deep cloak of crimson velveteen flowers?

And there's Turkish Delight, rose-petal jam,
water for cakes, rice, pies, worship of the Gods.
Added to salad, wrapping butter, steeping in brandy.

Dionysus loved a nymph whose beauty inflamed him.
Escaping she tore her dress on a thorny bush
with all her beauty revealed he loved her the more.

From her perfume and innocent blushes he created
the fragrant, red flowers the bush has borne ever since.

Anthony Fisher

Katherine as Tutor

I first met Katherine at Barnet College Creative Writing class over twenty years ago. I'd always enjoyed writing and she encouraged me in such an enjoyable manner that over the years, I gained enough confidence to enter competitions and submit short stories to magazines and the joy of winning a prize or having a story published has never diminished but I would probably have given up long ago without her ongoing help and guidance. I now attend a workshop she runs monthly in Barnet and still find her help invaluable.

Thank you, dear Katherine, with all my heart. I just hope you are aware how much you are loved and respected by so many.

Rosemary Fisher

Parallel Process

It could have been Queensland, a tree-house studio,
a tea-room quaint with doylies and china: imagine,
in the heart of the Daintree. Watching shadows play
at night, leaves brushing against the tarp; waking
to the early morning screech of galah and parakeet.

Do you remember the bindweed we threw across
the creek, like Tarzan and Jane, to avoid the crocodiles?

It could have been canvasses and charcoal,
the slime of oils, the pungent turps, that drive
to recapture - over and over - until time slows -
and the air becomes silk and breathes itself -
and new life moves through you.

It could have been our child, who listened
entranced, all freckles and redblond curls,
as you told your monster tales, and a stingray
drifted over fluorescent coral, and baby sharks
played beneath the glass bottomed boat.

And if I'd missed the flight,
if I hadn't returned?

That life together we dared not risk,
dreams on in us - like a Golem
waiting for our command.

Viv Fogel

I chose this poem because it's about a very happy time I spent in Australia and about a life I could have lived there - and almost did. I resonate with Katherine's poems about the wildlife and nature of her homeland, which she describes with such passion and love. Maybe part of her is also living a parallel life?

When I workshopped the poem in the stanza group she spoke about the sounds that the galah makes and we went through naming other Australian birds. But galah seemed right with parakeet. Katherine is a generous and encouraging mentor, tutor and colleague and I appreciate her support.

Eucalyptus Marginata

A small beehive, domed, sun-yellow, singing, set
against blue cloud-free sky, and the field (oh, sorry –
the paddock – surely), green and chirpy, to catch
the eye – this bee label buzzing from the shelf –
(as I dash along the late night aisle) – go buy me
– buy me – buy me! Ah yes, I thought, for you,
KG – this jar of honey is just right for your tea:
a touch of Jarrah to please your tongue – its amber
flowing (but not too sweetly), with a taste of here
– eucalyptus marginata; ingredients – australian.
So, now, it stands, on display, among my homely
kitchen clutter (– ah, small red robin, on the twig,
adrift; my farthing wren; the chunk of oak; my
moors, my cliff, my harbour, oh seaside town…
all remnants of a northern girlhood long gone).
Uprooted, you and I, we move between obverse
antipodes; the incomers; that first ground abjured
never. And hence, your words a pledge, alongside
decades of writing London (and the world), you
invoke this land not forgotten – a summer creek;
the first bush dance; walking the Three-Chain road;
the great grandfather, Irish, who didn't strike gold;
the miners turned farmers, paddocks dried hard
under February sun; then father working his acres;
mother's garden shoes; the cicadas ever-tuning, and
always those tall gums shadowing the dam; always
the girl, grasping the mane of the bolting horse;
beside that river's edge, she eyes the rising flood,

the take of speeding currents, the stepping stones;
an inland realm – an alignment, held close – my
reference point, you write, for other landscapes that,
after thirty years, have multiplied my skies; and so,
KG, for you – this trace: this glass jar's lucent trove,
wild nectar transformed; anticipating your arrival,
and that moment when we'll again set to work (on
the page, the line, the maze), perhaps glancing out
to Melbourne rain, while I pour tea and you spoon
the honey – drawn from old forest, its trees rooted
deep, slow growing, straight – tall Jarrah – the rough
fissured bark withstanding fire for a thousand years,
its high green canopy of shiny leaves, abundance,
and carrying, at branch tips, the thickening clusters
of creamy flowers, honeybees hovering...

Sandy Fitts

Electric Psalms

For Katherine, remembering our reading at Shortlands - a small advice for wannabe, would be, almost and already poets, including me. You don't need it - your poems are all GO!!

Cyclists,
heads wagging to the jazz
beat of their legs,
knees apart,
baskets overflowing
with little dogs or kids,
one heave and they stream
through an impossible gap,
no brakes on an oma fiets,
so go!
     Traffic lights? Ha!
A toothpaste squeeze
between tram and lorry.
No lights? So?
Text as you ride?
     This is how
to find out
what your poem
wants to say.
This is how to match
the electric psalm
in your heart
to your tongue -
add a little risk
and go!

(An oma fiets - grandmother's bike - is a boneshaker, ridden by women, men and children with long enough legs in Holland.)

Kate Foley

Touchstone

Katherine is one of nature's encouragers: not merely giving "heart" to apprentice poets about their work (courage from French corage from Latin cor = heart), but in how she makes you look for the core (or heart) of a poem, and dumping the inessential, self-indulgent clutter that gets in the way. She's an inspiration, and, if imitation is the sincerest form of flattery, this is my imitative homage to one of Katherine's poems which I found, and still find, a revelation.

Your touchstone poem unrolls like Russian dolls
where memories discover their beautiful form,
Laanecoorie, your pantoum that first opens my ears,
its nostalgia proxying every childhood holiday
where memories discover their beautiful form,
kaleidoscoping their heart-bright tangle of angles,
nostalgia proxying every childhood holiday
at noon-tide by the silver-tongued sun-struck Lodden
kaleidoscoping their heart-bright tangle of angles,
January topsy-turvily brimming the mercury to bursting,
at noon-tide by the silver-tongued sun-struck Lodden
where birds and kids can't believe that living is so much fun
as they're zooming through summer's particle-accelerator
in your touchstone poem unrolling like Russian dolls,
their naked marvels braiding our DNA,
Laanecoorie, your pantoum that first opens my ears.

Lindsay Fursland

Drafting

When I brought a very prosy draft of a piece, you wrote "Look at metaphors. It could become a poem." The first extract below moved, after that, slowly into the second as I struggled with it – it felt as hard as giving birth!

Before:

>how you were noticed, lab boy
>helped to make good, night classes,
>scholarship to medical school, how
>your gold medals must have shone
>and your further honours
>
>how your brilliance didn't burn out
>but fired you into working miracles
>as a physician, energised your enormous
>clinical war load, your duty to support
>the nurses – frightening, you said,
>
>how you pioneered perinatal medicine,
>created teams to help the whole child,
>inspired students, inspired me to believe
>that history guides present endeavour,
>that medicine is an art not a science

After:

>Stories of his meteoric rise, child
>from a council estate, dazzled them,
>
>a shooting star in the earth's atmosphere
>trying not to burn up.
>
>Gold medals shone,
>casting shadows.
>
>He shed new light on the whole child
>but only partly saw his own,
>
>travelled through continents of ideas,
>a fresh universe,
>
>bridging islands of thought,
>lighting up students with his lectures

Ruth Hanchett

First Flight Lift-Off

We hold hands, warm fingers press
gently, press firmly, our journey
of discovery about to begin.
We smile at each other.
The plane taxies to the off.

Ostensibly we read, sight glides over printed
pages, over glossy ads, over gossip
columns, unseen to the window.
Not even the page-3-girl, if present,
could distract now. Now the jet engines scream.

Taut as our seat belts, hiding our apprehension
under our outward composure
we somehow know the unknown.
Caressing fingers stroke rhythmic reassurance
fore-play of mesmerical first flight.

We hold our breath. The power beneath us speeds.
Finger press harder – a moment unaccounted –
we are aloft! Free from the gravity drag.
Hands relax, squeezing satisfaction
out of this minute airborne orgasm.

Gwen Hartland

Out to Lunch

The way a poet
will pick up the book you hand her
and disappear

in the middle of a conversation
away she goes and you know
you're talking to yourself

rinsed clean by the immersion
she'll resume engagement
with the world and you

but something's changed
her eyes don't quite connect
her ear half listening

still tuned to a remote frequency
you could get her to agree
to that trip to the Hebrides you've

been on about
she'd think you meant
Hesperides

where lunch beneath the
dappled shade
would be golden apples

Joy Howard

55 Douglas Road

Nadia wears her fake fur
like a buzzard.
Fine bone china cups
rattle open mouthed
back onto their saucers.

Tea cups filled, emptied,
washed, filled, emptied.
There's not enough china
for one sitting. The house
bulges with the conversations

that loosen with the black ties.
Sandwiches and cake
whipped in and down
and all the while
we stand like children.

Then you ask, 'But where
are the grownups?'
'We are the grownups,'
I say as the crockery
starts to break on itself.

Sonia Jarema

I love the way Katherine always has a twinkle in her eye. She is like a mother bird and has helped many fledging poets take their first scary but exhilarating flights from poetry-branches.

Spelling Katherine

I'm eating millefeuille in Loutro, dear Katherine.
Yesterday I was feeding the black fish cake.
The cicadas are singing if you can call it song
but real Greek music's strumming across the bay.

We've grown older I hate to say, dear Katherine,
though every time I see you, you're just the same.
I'd invite you to coffee if you were here.
You were so kind to me in our younger days –

'Fair Katharine and most fair' as Henry had it
or the Greeks before him: Aikaterina,
Aikaterinē – your middle e brought back,
and first recorded, after the Crusades.

Many Happy Returns, dear Katherine,
in any script or spelling of your name.

Mimi Khalvati

And

and then the platform's empty
and the train's pulling out
and she tries to run alongside
and bang on the windows
and her legs won't move
and someone is singing Que reste-t-il de tout cela
and a sign says Sortie
and she knows it's time to leave
and she still has his book
and the pages are uncut
and his words are unread
and the question is ...
and she already knows the answer
and that is now the end, she thinks
and then the strange thing happens
and a voice says write your own
and that is her beginning
and a luna moth settles on her wrist
and spreads its luminous green wings

Angela Kirby

From *A Scent of Winter*, Shoestring

To the Blue Gum in a London Garden

They brought you here from the nursery
as a spindly midget in a pot small enough
to sit comfortably on the front doorstep.
They couldn't guess a natural growing height
of 50 foot above the roof, a girth surpassing
cathedral columns, nor your bad habit
of casting limbs for no apparent reason.
How they loved your baby's-fist leaves
glowing blue in morning light, didn't know
they'd turn grey-green, grow long as giants'
fingers, ooze eucalyptus on any sunny day.

Now you stand stooped beneath a drab
London sky yearning for blueness, wideness,
and scarlet banners at day's end. You miss
Australian voices with their frequent oaths.
As you peep through a window to watch
football on TV, you long for soaring marks,
punt kicks and a score measured in goals
and behinds. You'd kill for a lamington.

Poor you, you can't take the tube to Heathrow
and fly home – but then again, why not?
Some people carry oak trees on the tube.

Kaye Lee

Once, long ago – as all the best stories begin – I went to my first poetry workshop. I didn't know the tutor from Adam, or should that be Eve, or perhaps Sheila, so imagine my delight on hearing someone speaking my language! And so began my long journey into poetry with you, Katherine, leading, guiding, encouraging me every step of the way. It's a journey I'd never have dared take on my own and one you have made so enjoyable – and to thank you here is my 'tree poem'.

The Policeman's Secret Notebook

I was imagining the wife's sherry trifle
when he flashed past me
      like a bolt of lightning.

December 23rd, sixteen hundred hours,
and not a sausage on him.
Just a pink tea cozy

pulled tight over his head.
I thought I was seeing things.
He ran so fast, I felt the draught

tickle my moustache as he shot off
into the Gents. And a lingering
smell of pickled herring.

He's still in there now.
He could be dangerous.
He might have a weapon concealed.

The station tells me they're streakers –
that they do this sort of thing
to cause a stir; for a bit of a thrill.

Well, let me tell you,
when I get my hands on him
he's not going to be disappointed.

John Mackay

Unarranged

It's cold now in this gaunt unheated house
so cool and clean in summer
when we first came
after the drums and the dancing,
the red thread, the sudden lifting of the veil.

In the summer we gave each other room
let cool breezes circulate
walked on tiptoe
until the white space
between our bodies filled with colour.

Now it's winter but heart's ice is thawing
now it's snowing but our blood runs warm
as in the dark stretches of long nights
we learn to make fire.

Tracey Martin

In Praise of Lazy Rivers

Shallow and frivolous, braided rivers
    spread and splay, beguiling me
        flaunting uncountable channels

like floozies or boozers, long hair in tangles
    silk robes floating open to negligées
        gathering buttered crumbs on thighs

Give me slow rivers anytime, their only job
    to shine and reflect patches of blues
        embroider clouds in silver-threaded doubles

I love the way they pay no mind to power
    refuse to rush or squeeze
        through chutes
        like all those
        touristic
        rock-
        licking
        waterfalls

Lazy rivers have the leisure given them
    by wide plains, the space to deposit their silt
        like swept lines of sawdust in a gymnasium

where dozens of dancers sway
    in calisthenic unison, ribbons floating
        from boneless wrists

Braided rivers say we have no need
    to choose between water and ground
        we can simply meander

let the earth show through now and then
    ridges of stones as clavicles, ribs and tibias
        spines and skeletons of long-ago streams

Nancy Mattson

At The Lifeboat Station (Early Evening)

On the gangway high above the water
I paused and looked back towards the shore

the whole beach was empty, but for two teenage boys
sprawled, lobbing pebbles at a disused wooden pallet
that they must have set on fire

jagged and transparent, blue and orange flames
were travelling the slats and cross-struts of its frame
like the hands of a swift experienced masseuse
(the waves, by comparison, seemed sluggish, overweighted)

The bigger boy glanced up as if conscious of my gaze
defensive, expecting a shout or an objection

but there was no danger, nobody was harmed
there was no-one else around

simply a nailed-together wooden structure burned
and a patch of shingle blackened.

Mary Michaels

Sprouts

It's good to be unimportant and watch time
sweep back, to repeat to the child starting school
that he's not going to die and not to think
about your own reasonably closer hour.

It's good to stride into the slap of winter
and let thought return the harvest of the little
cousin to the cabbage. It has a bud head,
a tight whorl of green that is its body.

O that delicious bitter of fresh-picked sprout
which, the Turkish green-grocer insists,
no one wants after Christmas. Aging,
it ruffles around the edges and turns yellow.

The next door neighbour can't be buried
before Christmas. The child wants marmalade
and butter on both toasts. I'm going to steam
my Brussels. The steam lays down a veil of frost.

Joan Michelson

Kennings for Katherine

Word weaver
Globe traveller
Foot soldier
Poem grower

There are some souls we meet, like tigers on the Silk Road
that make us wish we could all be a circus apprentice, like her

No sleepwalker, this, at the carnival's edge
encircling eye like fish rings on water

She catches each silver fin, tail flick, rhyme and ripple
picks them out, every one a passenger to the city
where walls are made of verse and every door
has her name on it,
Katherine

Joy juggler
Julien's mother
Stanza nester
Poetry jester

Cheryl Moskowitz

Here and There

That first year I travelled like a tourist,
agog at the opera house, the giant fruit bats
in the botanical gardens, and the calm
of mile after slowly changing mile as I drove

under the singing skies, skies that redefined
my sense of space, redefined the colour blue
and what it could do for the human spirit.
Blue fairy wrens and blue satin bowerbirds

were my new companions. The stars
were doubly bright, and when two of them
formed eyes above the smile of the moon,
what could I do but smile in return?

It was three weeks in when the simple road
through the goldfields became a muddle
and I stopped, lost. Above me, a cockatoo
perched on a bare branch, mocking my search

for a sign. Maldon was all I asked, but map
and plan were no longer in accord. The run
of perfect, adventurous days had given way
to the tiresome quotidian, reason for turning

back, accepting that travel is rarely more
than a provisional life, reason though too
for believing that a new world could be
home like the old, the old like the new.

Paul Munden

Katherine's Interview

This is part of our interview originally published in the International Notebook of Poetry No 8/2007, Poems in Translation: East and West. Essays on Poets and Poetry. I believe this fragment fully illustrates not only the core of Katherine's work but also, and most importantly, the essence of her spirit: a cosmopolitan individual always shaping and reshaping identity as a woman and a poet living in an effervescent, multicultural postmodern world.
May you keep travelling on in the spirit, my dear friend, and take us with you in your adventures!

I would say that all my poetry can be seen as a quest for identity and belonging, a move away from a dividedness, what Jo Shapcott calls the 'fractured sensibility'. This lifelong seeking after identity is no doubt true of most poets but probably more so of those who for some reason are living outside their birth country. Further, poets who happen to be women face an extra difficulty – that of writing within a still predominantly male poetry tradition.

I think the fact of having lived in France (1971-79) and travelling widely in Europe (which from an Australian point of view includes the British Isles) has helped me to perhaps feel less alienated by contributing to my sense of being a nomad – as if that were a proper condition in itself, my becoming a sort of wanderer-witness moving from place to place and, as if belonging nowhere in particular, apart from my homeland. One feels the loss but it is somehow divided into various places (the 'multiplied skies' of Hybrid) where one finds happinesses and consolations as one gradually becomes global and a citizen of the world.

My poetry is an attempt to come to terms with this divided sensibility. My decision to stay in Europe was very difficult. One does not realise what one is abandoning but finally, reality kicks in. Hence the need to grasp out for the lost paradise in memory. Of course, one never finally leaves it behind, but it too has changed. Who was it said, 'You can never go home'. It will have changed. But so will you. That is the paradox. Of course, coupled with the sense of accepting and valuing hybridity, is a recognition of travelling on in the spirit, if not in the sense of physically moving from place to place.

Becoming a poet is a slow but challenging, unending process. And there is so much to read. This is both the joy and burden of it. But if I were to start it all over again, I'm sure it would still be poetry first. It has given me so much – a way of seeing, a way of life. From where I stand now, the idea of not writing poetry is unthinkable. Sometimes I remind myself that I came to write it by accident. What if I'd missed out? Well, there's no answer to that.

Ironically, I began my writing career with short fiction, which I kept up in parallel with poetry until the mid 1980s when due to financial and time-pressures, I had to choose between them. Poetry was my first love...

Above all, poetry has given me a space of identity and belonging. As British poet Moniza Alvi said, "For Katherine Gallagher it is poetry, rather than her native Australia or her adoptive England that is 'this country you keep coming back to/that walks you home to yourself'."

Elena Nistor

For Katherine Gallagher, poet, teacher, translator, prime celebratrix
of road travel over the Himalayas, herewith a

Sonnet for Katherine

Ylang ylang
clan élan
the nostril caves
that breathe stars in
and charm to Spring
the air du temps
tune wombs to sync
turn brut men on
Sir Right, so wrong —
scent, women's sense
its hunters gone
nota its influence
nose does not close
adieu sagesse

Les Murray

Zigzag Thinking

Plath, you had the devil with you when you wrote,
scribing your perceptions and precise phrases,
stabbing them on to the pale paper.
Paper crying with the fiery observations,
hurting with the hurt.
Salved by the burnished clarity of words
beaded next to words they have never known
until poem necklaces glisten
with images that hang you with a tight choke
and leave you gasping.
Poems that smoke the mind and
leave small bonfires burning.

Did he sit beside you, pulling and
pushing at your thoughts?
Did he cook you breakfast?

Annmarie Nicholson

A Calculation of Dark

In this ruined light – the dark leaking into the garden
as if the light were an interloper

whose presence, no longer desired,
is sequestered to other places – the urgency of shadow

conspires, determines cross-woven words that lie
in the gap between desire

and undisclosed restraints.
Such absence is mocked by the schack-schack of jay

concealed in the elderberry beyond the boundary wall
but a quiver of leaves betrays

as will a breath, caught,
or the silk-split of a leaf loosed from its stem.

Ruth O'Callaghan
Published: The Shop

This Instant

the honeyeaters' cries pierce light...
the grevillea spikes are trembling
with flickers of bird
maybe, maybe,
sipping at spider-flowers
head down, grey and yellow.
Even here, gold and its shadow:
at the grass-roots level
the weeds are takeover bids;
at the end of the day
the bees choose mergers;
a butterfly floats
its banner against Monsanto,
orange and black like a dying sun
pushed up against bars.
B sharp, shriek the little birds, B sharp,
the edge of survival tastes of honey.
Listen:
two ring doves hidden in green
obsessively auditing peace.

Jan Owen

Congratulations, Katherine, on a fine body of work over the years! Your quickness, intensity, warm engagement, and presence -- at first meeting and at every meeting since -- puts me in mind of birds such as these honeyeaters.

tab:12

Earlier,
same night,
the first day.
Dusk.

A rhythm, rising up
through untried skin,
rhythms rising and falling,
a sense of mild disturbance,
rhythm, rest, rhythm.

Above the steepled spruce,
a blue dragonfly
waits,   darts.

Down,
down,
and
down, through wells of pitch,
down through the ripped suet
of the mantles of the boughs,
moves a milky phantom,
muttering to itself.

One foot crunches in front of the other, toe to heel,
track no wider than a handspan,
pigeon-steps in a rabbit track,
rebated through the umber chaff of the forest floor.

Pigeon it is. Lost.
Telling wishes to the trees
in the half-light.

Laurie Evan Owen

This extract from my novel *Kinch* is fondly dedicated to Katherine, a subtle and brilliant poet whose warmth, integrity and passionate commitment to her craft have been truly inspirational. The extract concerns Pigeon, one of the novel's main characters.

Katherine and Acumen

Katherine's first poem in Acumen was in issue no 1, a beautiful poem depicting autumn fires and music followed by the rebirth of spring. This early poem, full of a careful craftsmanship which never intruded itself onto the reader, was the first of many over the next thirty years. Another early poem was one about the birth of her child; twenty-five years later I published a poem about a wedding and wondered if it was the same one. Actually it was about someone else, but it brought home to me how long Katherine had been contributing to the magazine.

I have been publishing her poems at intervals through the lifetime of Acumen and she has taken me on some wonderful poetic journeys. Her sense of the natural world; her journeys of discovery both actual and imaginative, visiting people and places, all have been written with skill, sensitivity and an imaginative dimension which has lifted the poem off the page and sent the words scuttering off into the poetic soul of the reader.

I remember, without having to check, the poems about travelling to England, her thoughts on English gardens, crossing Asia, her relationships with family, friends and other poets. Katherine also read at the Torbay Poetry Festival where she delighted an audience with her poems about her journey from her native Australia and her wry views on her adopted country.

Thank you Katherine for your poetry and support over the last thirty years.

Patricia Oxley

Field Cricket and Poetry

placings
infinite strands of possibility
that must be planned,
white galvanic figures
on a chessboard of squareless green,
then the developing duel
of batsman/bowler
men who are stand-ins of the gods.
Whacked sound and thunder
of fast approaching feet,
and sometimes a red cannonball
to splay three soldiers at a time –
or from the sizzling
outer-works of skill, a whitewashed
dusty crease, is repelled
to boundaries of agreed infinity,
on deeply green ground,
nature-approved, where thousands
or a few watch.
A small enactment of pretended
greatness, a ritual and a test:
something like poetry.

William Oxley

The Other Side of the Bridge

Down from the road's rush of tyres
at the side of the bridge
there's an old set of steps,
each aged with grass and weeds.
Six, none quite the same,
their worn irregularity a work of art.
The seventh, eighth and ninth are triangles
turning towards the reed-lined water,
to reflections, breeze broken into thoughts.
The metal handrail turns with a twist of rust
beside a dandelion marking the bend
where the air rests softer
on the time-traveller between two worlds.

Dorrie Pearton

Barrier

flight over Cairns, Australia

In thin flat hues we see it drift
past the porthole – borne beneath us
on a microscope-slide of ocean:

amoebae of greener blue frilled
with the white fibrillae of surf – or
is it bright sulphate in a Petri dish

precipitating brown pancakes
of copper? Inorganic. Organic.
Images can swing both ways

for this hybrid of germ and rock,
these rods and spits of yeast
and bacillus. This is Life

made all the more strange
for being viewed from two
billion years up the food chain

through a lens of travel. Zoom in
and trigger-fish suck each tiny jelly
from its coral cup. Zoom out

and satellites make a thin
uneven curve that puts Australia
in parenthesis. Yes – we can

do all that. But this is our future
on a thread. A glimpse of our
Earth-child learning its chemistries

with no one to teach the lesson.

Katherine: stepping into a room, you're always a slice of summer. Your generosity: a perfect circle; your honesty: so plainly bright for those who dare peer into it. Unpretentious and honourable you are, in word and deed. Live long, Katherine; prosper!

Mario Petrucci

Young Katherine Meets Young George Meadows At The Poetry Society, Earls Court

Hello, I'm George Meadows,
I loved your poem in Poetry Review.

Thank you, I'm glad you liked it.

Yes, I really did. I understand you're from
down under. Where exactly?

Melbourne, do you know it?

I know Melbourne well... the bar
at the Windsor Hotel is magnificent.

What did you like about my poem?
Have you read much Australian poetry?

No not much, but I like yours.
It didn't go on too long. Also, I liked the way
you described sheep and wild lupins.
I think they're edible – have you ever eaten any?
Let's sit down comfortably?
That's much better. Come closer.

Are you sure you've read my poem?
My poem was about...

It was definitely yours, Katherine.

George, is that your hand on my knee,
because if it is, I think I'd better give it back to you.

Oh, let it stay a little longer,
it's really enjoying itself.

George, it's a very nice hand
but I think you need it more than I do.

Peter Phillips

Travelling Companions

He was so still, I didn't notice
when I sat down next to him.
I was reading my paper. Then
round the corner of the page, I saw
a clawed, grey paw.
The red jacket's collar was a furred neck,
headphones neatly looped around his long ears
long snout, jawful of big teeth and red inside –
gums, tongue – all as they should be.
I looked down. My shoe was touching
a large grey foot with curved black claws.
He didn't ask where I was going.
He got up at the next stop. He didn't
howl or bite or scratch. Silent, unassuming,
he got off quietly. No-one made any comment.
The first time I've sat next to a wolf on the 59 bus.

Not a Compliment

Elder to elder
teachers, poets
recognition across time
your years of work
some years of work together,
Salute to creative enterprise
the eye on the opportunity
critical standards
no nonsense Aussie welcome
the focussed passion.
Thanks and love, Katherine

Harriet Proudfoot

Cycle Race

We lean into the apex,
brace to accelerate. Bay windows
blur, reach out to hedges'
leafless bristles. We flow.
Cheering hits my ears,
somersaults in the slipstream. I
glance around: ahead
a kaleidoscope of bobbing vests
like popcorn on heat.
I don't see his veering
arc closing, my muscles putty,
pump-primed from this
sprint. I just don't see him,
can't decelerate.

Tom Roberts

Wake

This is world as you
believed in it once
and then again lying
in the grass you lay
flat and squinted sideways
so bright so clear the grass
with the sun in it
you believed you could and could not
enter and now the memory
that little cake
is delicious
everything gaudy and green
making your mouth water
and your toes curl.

Fiona Sampson

For Katherine

Kookaburras may fly in and out of her poems,
Australian as she is in her ways.
To all who know her, she is kind and supportive,
Hopes that we are all 'in it to win it'.
Energy she has in abundance,
Readings and workshops she gives and attends,
Imagination, her delight and resource to share with all.
Not for her taking it easy when there's more to do.
Eyes, her eyes, twinkle with warmth and mischief.

And all the other letters that would announce
the way she gives of herself, without artifice,
show or fuss, so that next time we need,
we ask again to drink from her generous pool.

Marina Sanchez

Katherine's Red Beret

fires us up as we arrive
in the Torriano's chilly room.
Katherine greets us,
her welcome's warm.

We lean on creaking tables,
tilt on wobbly chairs,
chew our pens and scribble,
hope our work compares

with others' brilliant efforts
rolling smoothly by
when our disordered verses
refuse to even try,

use split infinitives
and abstract nouns,
enter on a Journey
where cliches all abound.

So we leave it up to Katherine
to handle all our woes,
to make some calm suggestions,
introduce controls,

and when she puts her beret on,
and all our work is done,
we wander off to Kentish Town,
Poets, every one.

Daphne Schiller

Katherine

I first came across Katherine many years ago when I reviewed her book *Fish-Rings On Water*. I was delighted to discover not only her work but that there was another poet living not far away from me. We have been in touch ever since.

What I value about Katherine's wide-ranging poetry, is the frank way she treats personal experience, her sensitive poems about her parents and childhood in Australia and her sharp responses to contemporary life and world issues. I admire too the different tones she uses: ironic, witty, lyrical – feeling usually expressed through detail. She contributed a piece about her approach to personal subject matter for *Writing Your Self*, a resource book I co-authored with John Killick, and her contribution, which focused on her emotional life as a young woman, was invaluable.

Katherine is a tireless supporter of poetry and poets, a doer, not a self-promoter. For years she has run regular poetry workshops at the Torriano Meeting House in Kentish Town and also in Barnet. She has helped many develop their writing. Importantly, she started the Poetry Stanza Group for poets living in and around Palmers Green. She co-organized the Stevie Smith centenary festival in 2002 with Joanna Cameron, manager of the Palmers Green bookshop, and it is typical of Katherine and her interest in the work of other poets that she has continued to promote Stevie Smith's work, in particular by running workshops about her.

When Joanna Cameron put on poetry readings and other events at the Palmers Green bookshop Katherine and I helped her as much as we could. In 2006 after the owner closed the shop the three of us founded Poetry in Palmers Green which, with the help of a committee, puts on twice yearly readings, originally in St John's Church and more recently in the adjoining Parish Centre. It has been a pleasure to work with Katherine in programming each event.

There is a strong poetry community in Palmers Green and the area round it. Katherine, with her enthusiasm and determination, has played a key role in developing this. She deserves to be celebrated.

Myra Schneider

Les Salines, Normandie

At Les Salines
the sun examines every speck of sand

The sea takes another step back
then another

till the long straight lines
of the mussel farms come into view

The mussel-gatherers arrive on foot
with buckets and rakes

or driving tractors
with trailers and important dogs

At Les Salines
a cloudless sky reminds us

there'll be a few more summer days
like this, if we're lucky

The salt-grazers
potter past in a sheep-world of their own

The dunes sigh back another inch

Riders go by
on their sleek highbred Norman horses

The egret studies his reflection
in the shallow beck

The buzzard lolls
on his steep blue thermal

salt-sharp sun at his heel
at Les Salines

thoughtful neighbourly Les Salines
little sandy streets

of the salt-marsh town
folding their tourist tat away

for another year,
neat blue houses yawning their shutters down

Penelope Shuttle

In Celebration

                Your birth
           that sacred time
                    in south hemisphere spring
when your soul sang and was welcomed
by earth.

                         Your poems
                  glow and sparkle
                            like raindrops in sunshine
              held in the arms of a rainbow
                    they dance.

  To you
        wise and funny
    brim full of joie de vie
bold Scheherazade weaver of words
Sláinte!

Margaret Scott

In Flight

Cruising through cloud at thirty thousand feet
we are adrift, in limbo, feigning sleep.
We loll against the headrests, each as much
in our own dimension. Only turbulence makes us touch.

Mountains swim below us with peaks sharp
as fins. We manoeuvre round them. On one stark
wall two climbers hug their shadows on the ice,
minute, cheating gravity, limbs spread-eagled on the face:

perhaps they glance up at us, perhaps they smile
as we demean their skill, reduce their scale
with our engulfing bulk. And while our engines sing
we scoop their sunlight with our starboard wing.

Yet they thwart us: without their footholds on a ledge
our separateness would be supreme, our privilege
would be to scrape our fingers over rock,
trail avalanches through snowfields, make catastrophe, be god.

On the further side your daughter curls inside your arm.
Your face is young, like hers, yet softened, calm.
I am suspended here. In flight there is reprieve.
While her hand smoothes the whiteness of your sleeve.

Gordon Simms

The State Collection

'...the windows did not open the room to the world beyond, but framed
and hung the world in it like a picture.' *The Reader,* Bernhard Schlink.

Fixed under a pewter sky, Vienna's citizens framed
within a solemn arch. Breughel's Bird Trap encrusted
in timeless ice ...

The guard advances:

You must see Durer. She indicates, Below. I may comply
with her compulsion to direct disparate souls, on tight
itineraries, to the wonders of the palace ...

I could descend the stern stairway, traverse
the basement, find the café where a majuscule coffee
pot steams; where crenulated cakes sit like spikes.

Yet I remain

unresponsive to pleasure or to pain, pinned by familiar
iconography. From this arrow slit, this rim of time, I watch
the crowd mass, playful today

under the silent snow.

St Clémentin and Katherine Gallagher

In 2012 with plenty of ideas but no money Gordon and Jocelyn Simms
embarked upon the task of putting on a bilingual LitFest in the tiny village of
St Clémentin in rural France. We were delighted and surprised when
Katherine agreed to come and chair a poets' forum, put on a translation
workshop based on Jean Jacques Celly's epic, *The Sleepwalker with Eyes of
Clay* (Forest Books, 1994). Two years later she returned to lead a
workshop on Sylvia Plath and with festival friends presented a selection of
poems from *Through A Child's Eyes* (Poetry Space Ltd., 2013) translated into
French. Thank you, Katherine for your generosity, from Jocelyn, Gordon and
the St Clémentin LitFest team.

Jocelyn Simms

Nestlings

We're alert in the nest
shivering small wings.

We know we'll be fed
good protein, well sourced.

Feathers will strengthen
thanks to your care:

time taken from soaring,
from singing, from rest -

you as the phoenix,
food given as love.

Belinda Singleton

I've known Katherine for 20 years: a benign, talented, friendly, unpretentious face on the scene - can't think what poem of mine's good enough for her...
On St Nicolas' day in Holland, where he's known as 'Sint' (Sinterklaas), you write a (funny) poem for a family member and present a small gift with a connected theme. The poems are read out by a suitably clad 'Sint'. This is my only poem with an Australian connection - pretty clichéd - hope it will raise Katherine's forgiving smile...

The Reindeers' Revolt

(for Lily, my grand daughter, when about to spend Christmas in Oz)

Not this year Sint, we draw the line
a hoof too far, that friggin' time-zone flyin'

and when you finally arrive
a bloody heat wave, roasting you alive

your antlers start to melt, the reins
stick to your fur, no deer with any brains

would want to mix with kangaroos
ears bent by kookaburras, didgeridoos

and the carols! That Aussie verse
'The first day of Christmas...' it gets worse:

'... my true love sent to me, an emu
up an old gum tree...' We're through!

And are they sitting round a tree
sipping sherry, having a cup of tea?

They're not: XXXX in hand, half-starkers
they're on the Bondi Beach, looking for shark as

if this weren't the Good Lord's birthday
but some remake of Jaws. Sint, no way!

Get there on Qantas, and if they're on strike
Malaysian Airlines, hell, just go by bike!

And as for Lily, just make sure
She knows their climate, what she's in for.

Rudolf knows what sun can do
to noses, she needs protection too -

this prezzy's not beyond my income...
See ya Sint , yer onya tod – fair dinkum!

(My gift to Lily was a tube of sun tan lotion)

Hylda Sims

My Katherine

Oh, Katherine, my Katherine,
champion of the word,
oh, freshener of the daisies in my soul,
does not the elemental world lift its eyes to you?
Do not the skies, in dental fashion, open wide
to shine their light for you?

Oh, Katherine, my Katherine,
see-er in this wordy world,
oh, maker of my broken verses whole,
may roses lift their skirts to prance a pas-de-basque for you;
your muse skip on, forever brightly,
through the years with you.

Oh, Katherine, my Katherine,
pray, continue shining, as you do.

Anne Stewart

Dear Muse ...

(With thanks to Katherine Gallagher and her workshop on Stevie Smith)

Dear Muse, it's too early on a Saturday morning and I'm sitting here
at this writing workshop, tired and blank, waiting for you to appear.
Stevie Smith poems, two Gypsy Creams and one coffee (hot and wet)
have not been enough to entice you - at least, not as yet.

The week gone by fills my brain with concrete.
The week to come fills my heart with rain.
This Saturday morning – a clearing in the woods –
seems space and time too brief to tempt you in again.

Dear Muse, let's sit quietly together, this day, this week.
I will be ready to hear you, when you are ready to speak.

Christine Vial

For Katherine

Your talent for teaching is a joy that has led me though the wilderness of
creative writing.
Your suggestions have guided me along a path to improvement motivating
me to have the confidence to continue.
You are my mentor, my friend and my confidant on the 184 bus.
For all this I thank you.

Rita Walsh

Katherine Gallagher's Poetry

Much as I'd love to write about Katherine the lively, generous 'ideas-person' who has worked hard as a committee member of the Second Light Network, I want to focus here on Katherine the poet. She's a true original, a one-off. Her most exciting poems are not easy to categorise, successfully bringing together elements that are almost opposites.

She is a fine lyric writer with a light touch and underlying seriousness. There's an 'edginess' in much of her work but often combined with joie-de-vivre and optimism. Some poems bring together passionate feelings with a crystal-clear rationality and detachment. This kind of creative tension underpins some strong relationship poems. Katherine is demonstrably a cultured, sophisticated writer but a 'feet on the ground' element is there, reminding us that this poet's origins are in big, climatically challenging Australia where 'nous' is needed for survival.

Katherine's 'exile' from her home country and the adoption of two countries and cultures, France and England, is the kind of challenge which hones an edge. Living away from her roots was voluntary in Katherine's case, but is this so different from enforced exile? There have to be poignant memories, distance from family, questions about full integration / acceptance elsewhere, anxiety about eroding the first cultural heritage.

Katherine has returned to Australia relatively often and she has a substantial following and reputation there. There's ample evidence in her work that the thread hasn't been broken. In the fine poem 'Laanecoorie' (*Circus-Apprentice*) the Aboriginial name-place 'Laanecoorie' is used several times as part of the insistent music of this poem based on childhood memories –

"carrying with us always the mud and the stones and the memory
of Laanecoorie on the Loddon, with its long Aboriginal name;
aware only of the day, the heat of sun, the cool of water –
the Loddon, fringed by stout red gums, with their knotted roots."

I find myself conflating those 'knotted roots' with the poet's own attachment to her country. This poem and others draw emotional strength from sharp memories of 'time past' ("Looking back forty years, two brothers and a cousin lost to Lethe"), also our awareness that the poet has been torn from the heat, the smells, the flora/fauna of a landscape she can't (doesn't want to) get out of her system.

'Losing' one beloved landscape may make you especially aware of others. The pleasures of landscape and gardens and the need to save the planet are important themes in her work. Thinking about migration may also morph into thinking about our transit through life itself. She seems highly conscious of this analogy. Frequent references to travel in her work exploit layers of meaning. 'Flying' in a Gallagher poem may refer to daring, ambition, 'hat-over-the-windmill' stuff. One of the most exciting subliminal messages of her work is her deep-seated love of freedom.

'Confessional poetry' has been big for men and women poets during Katherine's writing career. Is she a 'confessor'? Strong poems refer to relationships including those articulating her mother's and father's personalities and lives. A major focus on desperate feelings would not be the Gallagher style but her work includes poems about exploitative sexual love. On a more general level, we can't miss that this poet is passionate and committed on many contemporary issues. She's also drawn to timeless subject-matter, including study of creative artists, especially painters and sculptors.

In the end what is significant about Katherine's work is its awareness and sensitivity. The distance from her roots, which she has obviously mourned, accepted and utilised, is the primary source (perhaps) of the sense so often conveyed in her work of the vulnerability of all people /peoples.

Dilys Wood

Intarsia

The dust of the material and spiritual
world awakes with surprise
in the cramped, crammed-full space
of a life's work.

"Look, my cousin, my brother,
a teacher - Rocco, my friend -
see them in the Stations
'the Way of Calvary'.

Figures walk out of their poses
assured of immortality,
nod to me, their feet joining
the torrent of footsteps spilling
from the archway of the Via Sersale.

I slip in through a side door.
Il Duomo dei Santi Fillipo Giacomo
is an arena for the theatre of Rome;
glistening with sun-splayed,
hand beaten chalices.

Haloed gods and goddesses
have their jewelled shrines;
stuccoed altars lit by musky candles
flickering into the eyes of supplicants,
drowsied by such solace.

Labourer's sweat trickles through
veins of marble pillars towering
above, taking the weight of centuries;
flakes of mother-of-pearl weep for back
rooms littered by hours of tradition.

Low chanting becomes murmurs from
the wood of past masters come to join
me, wrought iron screens shielding
their private prayers.

The Hesperides are here, head scarfed
embryo specs patterning the Nave -
the womb of this sepulchre.

Above our heads a dreamer's magnolia
heaven. The artist at my shoulder
stands back and checks his brush strokes
on this skin of eternity.

Artisans, artists, needle-worked fingers
stained with Pelican blood, crowd
around, each an exact piece of their own
creation - as yet unconsecrated.

I am fixed in my place,
a centre inside an inside -
the invisible world made visible,
arching and over-arching in scrolls
and whorls flowing from me;

a tree of life scattering splinters
of the unimaginable; rippling
vibrations of silence surpassing
conscious thought in the mystery
of the unexplained.

Wendy Wright

A poem for the artists Vicenzo Stinga and Allessandro Fiorentinto and the craftsmen
of Sorrento whose work can be seen in the Cathedral and the many churches of the area.
'Intarsia' is the Italian word for the craft of inlaid wood.

In the Company of Camels

The rug unfolded with the sun
(red orange green black).
Woodsmoke. The clink of plates.
From scattered sleep we'd meet
for night baked bread,
cake, jam, glasses of
Tuareg tea.

Acacias bleached bone white.
Sun dried dung. Flies.
Dates as tough as toffee.
In the scratchy midday shade
on the breadcrumbed rug
(red orange green black)
heat hung.

Wind smoothed evening dune.
First off the camels, the rug
(red orange green black)
an instant home on the rim of the world.
Had we all seen the mirage?
Tipped up in cosmic scales, the moon
shared the sky with the sun.

Now I roll out my memories
(red orange green black)
tasting the day warmed water.
The camels stray -
patterns on a kilim.
In the silk of today's sand
I'll tread again in their lily pad tracks.

Anne Woodford

Speedwriting

1.   Waiting for rebirth

At the funeral his old lover addresses him: you have been in the Bardo for 20 days loosening your soul from its old body and now, waiting for rebirth, you are frightened, excited, anxious, you are confused ... she tells him to be strong: and, if he is returning, to choose the womb wisely, give it his blessing, and only then, step in.

2.   A journey of starts

She thinks her life is this: beginning again, each time as if someone had put a cliff underneath her and she has jumped off: launched herself, starting again, and making some kind of landing, making a fist of it in any case. But now, this last cliff, she is flying off and flying off and, she is flying.

3.   Knowing it's a slow path

The twigs she expected but the bricks and other rubble, here in the middle of nowhere, as if some huge mansion, dwelling, city, town, some form of human habitation had been here all along and she hadn't known. And she is trying not to stumble: the doctor had said not to fall on her bad knee. You could damage the metal, dislodging it, and then what?

4.   Counting the signs

As children on long car trips they would play games. Here's one, she thinks: counting the signs: petrol stations or farm shops, say, or maybe the signs to their destination, each one bringing you nearer and closer, reeling you in.

B A Zanditon

Katherine

Many years ago, I was walking past Goldsmiths College and saw a notice pinned to a tree about a weekly poetry workshaop to be led by Blake Morrison. I immediately signed up for it, although I had not thought previously about doing such a thing. It was a wonderful adventure: he is an inspiring workshop leader. My background was visual art—I had never written poetry before and in the weeks that followed I became totally smitten with the reading, the writing of it.

One of the best things about the workshop: meeting Katherine Gallagher. We hit it off right away. Perhaps the fact that we were both "outsiders", growing up outside the UK — Katherine in Australia, me in America—had something to do with the mutual attraction. I was taken by her lively sense of humor, her kindness — and her total devotion to poetry. We have kept in touch throughout the years via letters and E-mails and meeting twice a month when we are both in London to go over our poems.

I owe her a great deal. Her suggestions for revisions are very insightful. She encourages me to take risks, to imply rather than state — and to write every day. And most importantly, I am inspired by her ingenious and arresting poems.

Katherine's hallmarks are a combination of spare, unpretentious words and a deep identity with nature: landscape, animals and — above all — human nature. Her poems also address important political and social issues that she feels strongly about.

She is a perceptive and original critic as well as poet, and a dedicated workshop leader who really cares about the progress of the poets who take part.

It has been my immense pleasure and honour to have been able to spend time with Katherine throughout the years.

Patricia Zontelli

Lost Property

the first room is all the odd socks,
dropped earrings, special Lego pieces,
the hook to the eye, the dress
that goes with the button you kept to remember

the second is what became of your schoolfriends
and the green eyed boy you loved at fourteen

the third is your dead mother, father, brother
smiling as if they'd never stopped

the fourth is that meeting in a wood
but this time your kiss works

the fifth is all the people
(laughing painting quiet dancing)
you wanted to be

the sixth is who you choose
out of all those people

in the seventh they give you back
all you never had

then there's the last

Veronica Zundel

Contributors

Shanta Acharya was born and educated in India, later studied at Oxford and Harvard. She has lived in London since 1985. The author of ten books, her poems have been published worldwide. Her collection, *Dreams That Spell The Light,* was published by Arc Publications, also Katherine Gallagher's publishers. Acharya's *New & Selected Poems* is due out in 2016. www.shantaacharya.com

Timothy Adès is a rhyming translator-poet, mostly from French (4 books to date), Spanish (one book), and German. He has four awards for translations, plus one for a lipogrammatic poem of his own. He runs a hand-picked, colourful bookstall of translated poetry at craft and gift markets. He is a member of the Poetry Society's Palmers Green Stanza, which Katherine leads.

Arc Publications was founded by **Tony Ward** in 1969, who remains its Managing Editor. **Angela Jarman** joined the press in 1993 as Editor. Arc publishes contemporary poetry from new and established writers from the UK and abroad, specialising in the work of international poets writing in English and the work of overseas poets in translation. Arc Publications have published Katherine's last three full collections.

Allen Ashley is a British Fantasy Society award winning editor, writer, poet, critical reader and writing tutor, currently running five creative writing groups. He co-hosts, with Sarah Doyle, "Rhyme & Rhythm Jazz-Poetry Club" at the Dugdale Theatre, Enfield. He first met Katherine Gallagher many years ago at Salisbury House Poets in Enfield and remains amazed at her dedication and energy.

Anna Avebury is a member of Ver Poets, St Albans. She began writing poetry seriously in 1995 and encountered Katherine Gallagher through Second Light Women's Poetry Network. She particularly remembers the poetry week-end held at Charleston, the home of Vanessa Bell and Duncan Grant, led by Katherine which was her first experience of Katherine's sensitive and imaginative approach to writing poetry.

Yvonne Baker (Govan) has been writing for several years and her poems have been published in numerous magazines, including Acumen, Envoi, The Interpreter's House and Orbis. Yvonne first met Katherine when she was a student with OCA and Katherine was her tutor. Katherine's encouragement and support gave Yvonne the confidence to continue writing at a time when she might easily have given up.

Anne Ballard has attended Katherine's workshops for many years, and the first draft of this poem 'Apology from a Reluctant Tortoise' was produced in one of them. Her poems have been published in various magazines and anthologies, she won first prize in the Poetry on the Lake 2015 Competition, and her pamphlet *Family Division* (Rafael Q Publishers) was published in 2015.

Michael Bartholomew-Biggs is a retired mathematician but a still-functioning poet and editor. He came to London from rural Bedfordshire in the mid-nineteen-nineties and very soon - probably via readings at the Troubadour or the Torriano - became aware of Katherine's work and her many contributions to the metropolitan poetry scene.

Liz Berry's debut collection *Black Country* was a PBS Recommendation, won a Somerset Maugham award and received the Forward Prize for Best First Collection 2014. She was a member of Katherine's North London Stanza from 2007-2012.

Barbara Bevan has known Katherine for more than thirty years both as a close neighbour and a great friend. The two families have been closely supportive throughout this time and Barbara looks forward with much enthusiasm to each of Katherine's many new publications.

David Bevan is a retired ecologist who was Haringey Council's Conservation Officer between 1989 and 2005. He is a past President of the London Natural History Society and the London Secretary of the Wild Flower Society. He is an experienced public speaker and has presented a number of recent poetry events including a celebration of the centenary of Dylan Thomas at which Katherine was a central contributor.

Rosemary Blake met Katherine in Australia in 2010 when they gave a reading together. They continue to meet when Katherine visits from time to time. Rosemary grew up in Australia but lived most of her adult life in Canada. Her work has appeared in Canadian, U.S., New Zealand and Australian literary publications and her poem "Time Zones" is from her collection, *Wintering* (Ekstasis Editions - 2007) She now lives in Australia.

Sara Boyes has produced two collections of poetry, *Kite* and *Wild Flowers* from Stride and a pamphlet, *Black Flame*, from Hearing Eye. She first met Katherine in the late 1990s when they gave a reading together on the South Bank. They now meet as participants in a poetry support group, an invaluable resource for getting a poem 'right'.

Ed Briggs lives in France working as a translator. Her poems have been commended by Hungry Hill and anthologized by Forward and Segora. In 2013 she won the Segora Vignette competition, and in 2014 was invited to judge it. She first met Katherine Gallagher in 2013 when attending a workshop in Normandy.

Maggie Butt first met Katherine through the National Association of Writers in Education (which Maggie chaired). She has taught Creative Writing at Middlesex University since 1990 and is a keen member of Katherine's Palmers Green Poetry Stanza. Her fifth poetry collection, *Degrees of Twilight*, was published in 2015 by The London Magazine and her first novel is due out in 2015. She is proud to count Katherine as a friend, and to be able to edit this anthology. www.maggiebutt.co.uk

Joanna Cameron's mother brought her up in London reciting poetry and literature to her and introducing her to people from around the world. Meeting Katherine through her job as Palmers Green Bookshop manager, Joanna has worked for the NHS, been a trustee of a complementary medical charity, and an Oxfam shop manager, hosting readers from Dannie Abse to Rowan Williams.

Rev. Franco Cavarra, is currently Parish Priest of St. Clement of Rome in Melbourne. Prior to his ordination in 1998 he had a long and varied career as a freelance stage director of opera and drama. In 2008, he staged a Way of the Cross for Sydney's World Youth Day seen on television around the world. He was a student of Katherine Gallagher's in 1964/65.

Kay Cotton lives in rural Normandy after raising a family and working as an Educational Psychologist. Offering poetry and music retreats and workshops with her partner Sylvia has become an important feature of life alongside sending poems out into the world. Katherine, with her joyful attitude has attracted participants over the years and has become a firm friend.

Martyn Crucefix has known Katherine as an inspiration in her commitment to poetry (that of others as much as her own) for almost 30 years. His publications include *Hurt* (Enitharmon, 2010), *The Time We Turned* (Shearsman, 2014), *A Hatfield Mass* (Worple Press, 2014). He has translated Rilke's *Duino Elegies* and *Sonnets to Orpheus* for Enitharmon. *Daodejing* – a new version in English is due in 2016.

C.L. Dallat, poet, musician, critic, (b. Ballycastle, Co. Antrim), lives in London, has written for TLS, Guardian, etc, and is a regular contributor on Radio 4's Saturday Review (since 1998). Winner of the 2006 Strokestown International Poetry Prize and member, with Katherine, of the seminal Robert-Greacen/Matthew-Sweeney 1980s/1990s workshop, his latest collection is *The Year of Not Dancing* (Blackstaff, 2009).

Valerie Darville, together with Anthony Fisher and the late Jane Elder founded Enfield Poets, formerly Salisbury House Poets. It was here they met Katherine who was a regular attendee and guest. Valerie has been placed in many competitions, including the Bridport twice. She compared shows at the Dugdale where guests have included Carol Ann Duffy, Ruth Padel and Andrew Motion.

Ross Donlon is an Australian poet who has enjoyed Katherine's hospitality & guidance when he comes to London. They help each other find readings, when each is in the other's country.

Penny Dopson writes as much as she can each week now she is retired, also works with friends and goes to regular writing workshops. She is passionate about poetry and belongs to Ware Poets. She first met Katherine in 2012 as mentioned in the poem. Since 2014 she has attended Barnet Writers Workshops led by Katherine to help her get more poems published.

Sarah Doyle is the Pre-Raphaelite Society's Poet-in-Residence, and co-hosts Rhyme & Rhythm Jazz-Poetry Club at the Dugdale Theatre in Enfield. She is a member of Katherine's Palmers Green Stanza, and has attended many inspiring workshops run by the great lady.

Jane Duran was born in Cuba, brought up in the USA and Chile and lives in London. She has written five books of poetry and co-translated Lorca's *Gypsy Ballads,* all published by Enitharmon Press. Jane first met Katherine at the Torriano Meeting House, and they each had a pamphlet published by Hearing Eye in the 1990s.

Margaret Eddershaw started writing poetry after retiring from university teaching in 1996 and met Katherine via Second Light. Margaret greatly appreciated Katherine's generous interest in a 'new' poet. This extended to her warm support for Margaret's four performance poetry shows (three seen at Torriano). Katherine and Margaret also share a love of sport – rare among female poets?

Pam Edwards BEM, has been Hon Sec of Barnet Borough Arts Council since 1965, except for a spell in Glasgow as administrator of Cumbernauld theatre and ten years developing The Bull Theatre in Barnet. BBAC links about 100 groups and artists across the Borough. Pam is also Chairman of East Barnet Festival.

Roger Elkin has won 45 First Prizes and several awards internationally, including the Sylvia Plath Award for Poems about Women, and the Howard Sergeant Memorial Award for Services to Poetry (1987). His 11 collections include *Fixing Things* (2011); *Bird in the Hand* (2012); *Marking Time* (2013); *Chance Meetings* (2014). Envoi Editor (1991-2006), he is available for readings, workshops and poetry competition adjudication.

Diane Fahey is the author of twelve poetry collections, most recently *The Stone Garden: Poems from Clare,* shortlisted for the Kenneth Slessor Poetry Prize. Diane, like Katherine, attended the University of Melbourne, and they met thereafter in the Melbourne literary scene and would often get together in the years Diane lived in London (usually also with writer Diana Sampey) to work on poems, always a valuable experience. So, friends in poetry – an ongoing gift. Diane's website is dianefaheypoet.com

Anthony Fisher met Katherine in 2000 at Salisbury House Poets (now Enfield Poets) which he founded with Valerie Darville and the late Jane Elder. Anthony was regular attendee at Katherine's workshops and she also mentored him. He has made frequent appearances at the Dugdale Theatre, notably alongside Carol Ann Duffy and Andrew Motion, and at other poetry venues around London.

Sandy Fitts was born in England and for most of her childhood lived on the Yorkshire coast, with time also in Surrey and Merseyside, before going to live in Melbourne, Australia. Her award-winning book of poetry *View from the Lucky Hotel* was published by Five Islands Press, 2008. Sandy and Katherine met in London 2000 and enjoy a friendship steeped in poetry writing, in both hemispheres.

Viv Fogel's poems appear in various anthologies and have been heard on radio. A psychotherapist for over 30 years, she teaches, publishes articles, gives talks, is too busy to enter poetry competitions but enjoys being asked to read! Her collection *Without Question* (2006) and pamphlet *Witness* (2013) are published by Mandaras. She met Katherine through the Second Light network of readings and workshops.

Kate Foley. Once a Londoner, now mostly an Amsterdammer, Kate Foley writes, reads, leads workshops between UK and Holland. T*he Don't Touch Garden,* her 8th publication, will be published by Arachne Press in September 2015. She'd bumped into Katherine at many a poetry 'do' but when she recently shared a platform with her at the Shortlands poetry festival she realized how much she appreciated the wise, witty and warm person and her poetry.

Lindsay Fursland lives in Cambridge where he runs the Poetry Society's Stanza, and also is involved in CB1, an organisation that puts on monthly poetry readings in the city. He has been attending one of Katherine's writing workshops for the past seven years, and thanks to her encouragement and advice has grown as a poet.

Ruth Hanchett met Katherine at 'Salisbury House Poets' in 2011 when, for the first time, she read some of my poems. Katherine encouraged her to join the Second Light Network for women poets and the Palmers Green Stanza Group: her poetry developed greatly from then. A late starter, she is now delighted to achieve some good poems and occasional public success.

Gwen Hartland joined the late Jane Elder's Creative Writing class in 1987. She became a member of the Enfield Writer's Workshop and of the Salisbury House Poets, where she first met Katherine, appreciated her poetry and the pleasure of her company. Now Salisbury House Poets has become Enfield Poets at the Dugdale Centre, Enfield, Gwen is still a member, still learning and improving, she hopes.

Joy Howard runs Grey Hen, a poetry press dedicated to showcasing the work of older women. She has produced six anthologies and a chapbook series. She met Katherine through her membership of the Second Light committee, and has published her poems in several of the anthologies. Katherine was an adjudicator of the Grey Hen annual competition for women poets over 60 in 2012.

Sonia Jarema was born in Luton to Ukrainian parents and now lives in Enfield. Her poems have appeared on-line in Ink Sweat and Tears, Every Day Poets and in print in South Bank Poetry, South, Envoi as well as in several anthologies. She has been shortlisted for various competitions and commended for 2014 Barnet Arts Poetry Competition. She is a member of Forest Poets. "Katherine Gallagher's monthly workshops at Torriano House were recommended to me by Myra Schneider and I loved them. Katherine really helped to build up my confidence, introduce me to a wide range of poetry and to sharpen my critical skills."

Mimi Khalvati has published eight collections with Carcanet Press, most recently, *The Weather Wheel*, a Poetry Book Society Recommendation. She started writing poetry in 1986 and met Katherine very early on in her writing life, particularly at gatherings at Torriano Meeting House. Katherine was already well-known and very encouraging to new writers whom she made welcome into the writing community.

Angela Kirby is a Lancastrian who now lives in London. Her poems are widely published and broadcast while many are translated into Romanian. Her collections from Shoestring Press are *Mr. Irresistible*, 2005, *Dirty Work*, 2008 and *A Scent of Winter*, 2013. A fourth is due in 2015. She met Katherine on the London poetry circuit where they soon became friends and together judged the 2013 Second Light Poetry competition.

Kaye Lee is an Australian living in London. She wrote poetry of sorts for many years but only had time and energy to take it seriously after retiring from nursing. This was when she started attending Katherine's workshops. She has since been published in magazines and anthologies and owes much of her development as a poet to Katherine's encouragement, support, and, especially, friendship.

John Mackay, poet and paronomasiac, was delighted to discover that all those misspent afternoons watching Countdown had paid off when Katherine invited him to take over the role of Treasurer for Poetry in Palmers Green.

Tracey Martin is a poet and development practitioner. Tracey was a prose writer until she did an Open College of the Arts distance course while based in Bangkok. Katherine was her poetry tutor on that course and inspired her to write poetry. When she returned to the UK she joined the Palmers Green Poetry Stanza that Katherine runs. She wrote this poem at one of Katherine's Stevie Smith workshops. "I wouldn't be a poet if it hadn't been for Katherine - long may she continue to inspire others!"

Nancy Mattson moved from Canada to London in 1990 and met Katherine soon after, at the Troubadour or Torriano, perhaps Australia House or Canada House. Anywhere poetry could be found in London, Katherine was there! The friendship, encouragement and poetic wisdom of a fellow 'colonial' have been invaluable to Nancy; her third full collection is *Finns and Amazons* (Arrowhead Press, 2012).

Mary Michaels has been writing poetry and prose poetry since the early 1970s. A writer always needs a reader who can be trusted to make objective critical comment before a poem is exposed to the public. Over the last decade, as fellow member of a small workshop group, Katherine has fulfilled this function. In return Mary has had the pleasure of seeing many of Katherine's own poems in the process of taking shape on the page.

Joan Michelson, *Toward the Heliopause,* 2011; First Prize 'Stories', Bristol Poetry Competition 2015; First Prize, 'Daxon Fraser', Torriano Poetry Competition, 2014; Writing Residency Awards, 2014 'Omi International, New York, The Virginia Center for the Arts'. "When I think of Katherine, I think of unfailing encouragement, support, dedication, energy and forward drive for members of the poetry community and to individual poets, myself included."

Cheryl Moskowitz is a poet, playwright and novelist. Like Katherine, she writes for children and adults. Her publications include the poetry collection *The Girl Is Smiling* (Circle Time Press 2012), novel *Wyoming Trail* (Granta 1998), and poetry for children *Can It Be About Me?* (Frances Lincoln Books 2012). "I have been lucky enough to be a member of Katherine's North London Stanza group for the past 7 years."

Paul Munden is Director of NAWE, the National Association of Writers in Education, and currently Postdoctoral Research Fellow at the University of Canberra. His book of new and selected poems, *Analogue/Digital,* has just been published by Smith|Doorstop. As general editor of NAWE publications, he worked with Katherine while she was a co-editor of Writing in Education.

Les Murray is an Australian poet, anthologist and critic. His career spans over forty years and he has published nearly 30 volumes of poetry as well as two verse novels and collections of his prose writings. His poetry has won many awards and he is widely regarded as the leading Australian poet of his generation.

Annmarie Nicholson met Katherine four years ago at a Palmers Green poetry reading where Katherine gave her a flyer for her Torriano workshops. "My reaction was yes, a published poet, I like her poetry, a positive woman, Australian and appreciative of Sylvia Plath's work."

Elena Nistor was born and lives in Bucharest, Romania. She met Katherine at the 2004 Second Light Festival in London, as a PhD candidate researching for her thesis on contemporary British women poets. Since then, their friendship has flourished. In 2012, her study received the summa cum laude honour by the University of Bucharest, and was published as *A Blossom of Words in a Dusty Ray of Light:* Contemporary British Women Poets (1950-2005).

Ruth O'Callaghan has six collections of poetry, is translated into five languages, is an editor, mentor, adjudicator, leads workshops in Lisbon and London and elsewhere in the U.K. She runs two poetry venues where the famous and not-so-famous read side by side. She and Katherine serve on the same committee.

Jan Owen is a South Australian poet whose most recent book, *The Offhand Angel,* was published in July 2015 by Eyewear. Her translations of *Selected Poems from Les Fleurs du Mal of Charles Baudelaire* was published by Arc in June 2015. Jan first met Katherine at a poetry reading in London in April 1989 and they have kept in touch ever since.

Laurie Evan Owen's childhood switched from Birmingham to the Chilterns. After grammar school and art school in Oxford, he studied painting at the Royal Academy, worked as an artist in London, married, worked as a house painter, divorced, moved to the Sussex coast and completed Kinch, his first novel. He met Katherine after joining the North London Stanza poetry group.

Patricia Oxley met Katherine through her poetry. She accepted several of her poems and when they actually came to meet she says she felt as if she had known Katherine for years. She is sure they met before she asked Katherine to read at the Torbay Poetry Festival, probably at a poetry reading in London.

William Oxley is a poet with many collections of both prose and verse to his credit. In 2014 his *Collected & New Poems* was published by Rockingham Press. He has given many readings both in Devon where he lives, and in distant places like the Cote d'Azure and Nepal. For many years he has frequently met Katherine Gallagher, whom he regards as a good friend and fine fellow poet.

Dorrie Pearton is a retired teacher and only started writing in the year 2000 thanks to encouragement from Katherine. Since then she has mainly used the natural world as a subject getting close to it because, with her husband, she enjoys trips into the countryside in their camper van.

Mario Petrucci. Ecologist, PhD physicist and Royal Literary Fund Fellow Mario Petrucci is a multi-award-winning poet, broadcaster and residency frontiersman, the only poet to have held residencies at the Imperial War Museum and with BBC Radio 3. He first met Katherine at a poetry gig in the Londinium drizzle of the eighties poetry scene, where they discovered they shared a somewhat similar, tanned disposition.

Peter Phillips is a London poet. His fifth collection was *Oscar and I, confessions of a minor poet* (Ward Wood Publishing, 2013). He's now writing a series of poems called *Saying it with Flowers*. He met Katherine at the Torriano poetry readings in Kentish Town, north London, which he has attended since 1994.

Harriet Proudfoot taught in Primary Schools and Higher Education. Her chapter, 'Development through the Creative Arts' was published in *The Primary Curriculum in Action, 1983*. She inaugurated Poetry at the Mary Ward Centre and taught Creative Writing there and at Morley College for nine years. One prize-winning student recommended Katherine's classes. Harriet has enjoyed and profited from them for several years.

Tom Roberts is a poet from County Antrim and has been published in magazines and anthologies. He knows Katherine from her great work for the North London Stanza. Its success is in no small part due to her organisational skills and calm manner.

Fiona Sampson recently published *Selected Poems* in the US, China, Romania and the Ukraine. She's received various national and international prizes and is Professor of Poetry at Roehampton University. She says, "I've known Katherine since I started working as an editor and have always loved her wry charm, at work both in the poems and in person."

Marina Sanchez. Before joining the North London Stanza, she'd known Katherine for years from enjoying her workshops. Since Marina joined the Stanza, she values Katherine as a hard-working, cheeky and inspiring rep. As soon as Marina's *Dragon Child* (Acumen), was published, it became Book of the Month for January and February in the Poetry Kit website. Read more in her poetry pf pages.

Daphne Schiller has been a member of Ver Poets since 1975, and served 10 years on their committee. Her poems have been published in magazines and anthologies and some have won prizes. She met Katherine Gallagher at Second Light events and went to several of her monthly workshops at the Torriano in Kentish Town.

Myra Schneider first met Katherine at a poetry reading in 1989. Myra's most recent collection is *The Door to Colour* (Enitharmon 2014) and she co-edited *Her Wings of Glass,* an anthology of ambitious poetry by women poets (Second Light Publications 2014). Other publications include books about personal writing. She tutors for The Poetry School and is consultant to the Second Light Network.

Maggie Scott is an eclectic poet, whose work covers a multitude of themes. However she often draws inspiration from the natural world and our place within it. Maggie has attended Katherine's residential retreats in Normandy and is a member of Torriano poetry group. She recently read at Torriano Meeting House. Maggie is working towards producing a pamphlet of her work.

Penelope Shuttle lives in Cornwall and is a poet and poetry tutor. Her next two publications are - *Heath*, a collaborative book-length sequence of poems inspired by Hounslow Heath, with John Greening (Nine Arches Press, 2016), and her twelfth solo collection *Will you walk a little faster,* Bloodaxe,

2017. She tutors for Arvon, and for Brantwood House in Cumbria, among others.

Gordon Simms was Head of Performing Arts at Blackburn University before retiring to France. Katherine Gallagher reviewed his collected poems which won the Biscuit prize (*Uphill to the Sea*, 2012). She kindly agreed to judge the Segora poetry competition of 2012 and results were announced at the first St Clémentin Bilingual LitFest of which Gordon is president. www.stclementinlitfest.com

Jocelyn Simms has lived in France since 2002. She organises annual Segora International writing competitions and a bilingual LitFest in St Clémentin to which Katherine Gallagher has given great support. Jocelyn's poetry about the Atomic bomb and subsequent testing on unsuspecting military personnel has recently been published by Hungry Hill, *Poets Meet Politics*. www.poetryproseandplays.com

Hylda Sims, South Londoner, writes novels, poetry and songs; has worked as folk singer, Elizabethan minstrel, skiffle singer, communard, teacher and single parent. She hosts a monthly poetry and music event, Fourth Friday, at the Poetry Cafe in London's Covent Garden, plays guitar and sings with skiffle & blues group, City Ramblers Revival. She lives in South London. Katherine has read at events she has hosted and vice versa over many years. hyldasims.wordpress.com

Belinda Singleton returned to writing poetry in 2008. Katherine heard her read in 2010, encouraged her to aim for publication and invited her to join the Torriano workshop group. She's still happily there. Belinda reads at London venues and is Chairman of Wey Poets at Guildford. Publication has been via poetry magazines, competitions and anthologies. A collection is due shortly.

Anne Stewart met Katherine Gallagher through Second Light in 2002. Interviewed in Brittle Star (Spring 2008), and nominating her (KG) as their next 'super hero', Anne said "chatting with Katherine Gallagher about poets being invisible" first planted an idea to combat it, which came to fruition in www.poetrypf.co.uk. Katherine was Anne's mentor in preparing her first and second collection(s). "Thank you Katherine."

Christine Vial is a poet who teaches literature and creative writing in North London. She first met Katherine through the Barnet Poetry Cafe and both are members of Palmers Green Poetry and Second Light. Katherine's enthusiasm, expertise and unwavering support for poetry and poets – no matter how humble – have been support and inspiration to her as to so many others.

Dilys Wood founded the women poets' network, Second Light Network (SLN), in 1994. Katherine Gallagher became a highly active member of SLN's committee, tutoring workshops, writing for ARTEMISpoetry magazine and judging the poetry competition. Dilys regularly co-edits ARTEMISpoetry, has co-edited six anthologies of women's poetry, the latest *Her Wings of Glass* and *Fanfare* (forthcoming), and has two poetry collections published.

Anne Woodford lives in Anjou where her interest in writing led her to the St Clementin literary festivals and Katherine Gallagher's vivid poetry. Anne's contribution, 'In the Company of Camels,' resulted from a trip to the Sahara. Other adventures – awaiting poems? - have included travelling overland to Vietnam, and researching family connections in Calcutta. "Thank you, Katherine, for your inspiration."

Wendy Wright met Katherine in the late eighties through Brenda Walker of Forest Books, who published *Fish Rings on Water* Katherine's first collection in the U.K. Wendy was often with her at readings, went on her poetry courses, became friends and recommended her for the Deux Sevres LitFest where she did a workshop on *The Sleepwalker with Eyes of Clay*, (Forest Books.)

B.A. Zanditon is a poet and visual artist. She has been in a writing group with Katherine for a number of years. These poems came out of a suggestion from Katherine at a recent workshop that some word pictures be used as the jumping off point for poems. They were written fast, hence the title.

Patricia Zontelli. New Rivers Press published Patricia's 1st and 2nd poetry collections; the latter, *101* was finalist for the US National Poetry Series. Her poems have been published in many US and UK journals and anthologies. Patricia and Katherine met at a poetry workshop many years ago and continue to this day to get together to "workshop" their poems.

Veronica Zundel is a freelance writer for the Christian market and a sporadically published poet. She first met Katherine through winning the Barnet Open competition in 2005, and now belongs to the Palmers Green stanza. She lives in Muswell Hill with a husband, a grown-up son and a very fluffy cat. Her blogs are www.reversedstandard.com